The Incredible January Effect:

The Stock Market's
Unsolved Mystery

The Incredible January Effect:

The Stock Market's
Unsolved Mystery

Robert A. Haugen
Boyd Professor of Finance
University of California, Riverside

Josef Lakonishok
Karnes Professor of Finance
University of Illinois, Urbana-Champaign

DOW JONES-IRWIN
Homewood, Illinois 60430

This publication is designed to provide accurate and
authoritative information in regard to the subject matter
covered. It is sold with the understanding that the
publisher is not engaged in rendering legal, accounting, or
other professional service. If legal advice or other expert
assistance is required, the services of a competent
professional person should be sought.

*From a Declaration of Principles jointly adopted by a Committee
of the American Bar Association and a Committee of Publishers.*

This book was set in Times Roman by The Saybrook Press, Inc.

The editors were Richard A. Luecke, Joan A. Hopkins.

The production manager was Carma W. Fazio.

The drawings were done by Alice Thiede.

Arcata Graphics/Kingsport was the printer and binder.

ISBN 1-55623-042-7

Library of Congress Catalog Card No. 87-70918

Printed in the United States of America

2 3 4 5 6 7 8 9 0 K 5 4 3 2 1 0 9 8

This Book Is Dedicated to Our Families

Acknowledgments

This book was completed while Haugen and Lakonishok were at the University of Illinois, Urbana-Champaign and Cornell University respectively. The authors wish to thank Angie Pitard for her administrative assistance. We would also like to thank Hal Bierman, Joseph Dada, Werner De Bondt, Tom Dempsey, Thomas Dyckman, Bulent Gultekin, Richard Haugen, David Ikenberry, Bill Kinney, Charles Kroncke, John Leonard, Charles Linke, Mike Rozeff, Sy Smidt, Richard Thaler, and Seha Tinic for their very valuable comments. A special thank you goes to the real Tiffany Meyer for very valuable editorial assistance. We would also like to thank Dick Luecke for his valuable assistance as our editor.

Contents

Only in January

This is a little book about something very BIG.

You may not have heard about it yet, but there are some mighty interesting things going on in the stock market. Moreover, these things have been going on for many, many years.

Strange things.

A real mystery.

Not just your plain, ordinary, run-of-the-mill, everyday mystery, either. This one's a tough nut to crack!

You're probably thinking, "If something this big has been going on in the stock market, how come I haven't heard anything about it or noticed anything?"

Because, even when something is this big, you can't see it in the major market averages like the Dow or the S&P 500. You see, the major market averages are dominated by the corporate giants like IBM and AT&T. And the subject of this book has its greatest impact on smaller companies.

Lots of people are trying to solve this mystery.

Now you might be thinking, "If lots of people have been trying to solve it, why haven't I heard of *them*, either?"

Because they live in ivory towers, and they don't come out that often.

For at least 10 years, literally HUNDREDS of university professors in the United States and throughout the world have been wringing their hands over the answer to this one. What's more, as their work reveals what is apparently happening in greater and greater detail—as the pieces of the puzzle slowly fit together—the mystery only deepens.

So what is the mystery?

In the stock markets, in the bond markets, here and abroad, some very funny things are happening. Things that defy a rational explanation. But they happen only in January.

There's something very funny about the returns produced by securities in January.

There's little that is odd or funny about security returns in the other 11 months of the year. You can buy the stocks at the beginning of each month, and you can sell them at the end. Your rate of return is your monthly income (dividend and capital gain or loss) divided by what you paid for the stock at the beginning of the month. Show us the pattern of returns produced by different stocks in December and April, and we won't know which month is which. The same is true for March and July, or any other pair from the 11 months remaining.

January, however, is clearly different.

Show us the pattern of returns typically produced in January, and we'll pick it out. We won't need fancy statistics to do it, either. The uniqueness of January will jump right out at us. And what we see defies apparent explanation.

For one thing, the average returns for a typical stock in January are bigger—*much* bigger—than the returns for the other 11 months. Typically MANY TIMES larger. This is not to say that returns in January are *invariably* large. At times they are not. At times investors even lose money in January. But take a reasonably long series of Januaries, say 20 years' worth. The average January return for the 20-year series is nearly always much larger than a comparable series for any of the other months. Surprisingly, the greatest chunk of return earned by investors is usually earned during a single month—January.

In short, if you are not *in* the market in January, you are *out* of it. At least you're out of the kind of market you probably expected to be in.

That's not all. The expected January bonus return isn't the same for all stocks.

As we said, one reason that the January Effect has taken so long to be discovered is that you can't really see it in the most widely watched stock market indexes. These indexes are nearly always weighted by the total market value of the stocks in them. Take 1 percent of the total market value of each of 500 companies, and you have a value-weighted index. Value-weighted indexes like the S&P

or the NYSE Composite are dominated by the big companies that take up the biggest shares of the indexes. Dow, the most popular index, includes 30 of the largest companies.[1]

And as it turns out, the January bonus becomes smaller as the size of the company becomes larger.

The common stocks of *little* companies get the lion's share.

Now, if you really look hard, you may find evidence of this same sort of thing going on during the other 11 months—little companies earning higher than average rates of return. But in these months the effect is slight. In January it is ENORMOUS. In January the average returns to the smallest companies' stocks is typically *10 to 12 times* larger than the returns to the largest companies' stocks.

BIGGER RISK, BIGGER RETURN

Stocks are pretty risky investments in general, but some stocks are clearly more risky than others. A typical investor wouldn't put an airline stock in the same league with the stock of a public utility. Since they take more risk with the airline, they'll prefer the utility unless the airline offers a higher *expected* rate of return. They want something extra to entice them to take a chance.

In finance they call this *extra* something a risk premium.

Risk premiums usually show up in the returns actually realized by investors. If we invest in airline stocks and you invest in utilities, and we wait long enough, we will probably earn a higher rate of return than you. We deserve it. After all, we took the chance; we expect to be compensated with more return. And, if events turn out pretty much as expected, we will be.

A reasonable person might think that risk premiums will be earned gradually or, for more risky investments, randomly, during the life of the investment. In any case that's what "experts" always thought.

It seems that they were wrong.

As it turns out, nearly all risk premiums are earned in a single calendar month. That's right, in January. You can expect to get the same returns from airlines and utilities if you hold them in any other month.[2] Only in January will the airline *usually* outstrip the return from the utility.[3]

Surprisingly, the same thing seems to be true in the corporate bond markets. You may have seen promised yields on bonds of different qualities in the financial press. These promised yields aren't quite the same as the expected or realized returns we've been talking about thus far. They call these promised yields *yields to maturity*. These are actually the returns being promised to you by the firms that issue the bonds. If you hold the bonds until the day they mature, and *if the firm is able to make all the promised payments*, your realized return on the investment will be the same as the bond's yield to maturity.

Now, in any given month, low-quality bonds always have higher yields to maturity than their high-quality counterparts. That's because investors recognize the greater probability of default on the lower-quality bonds. They require greater promised payments, because they don't really expect the promise to be fully realized.

If greater promised payments automatically mean higher yields to maturity, does this mean that we can actually expect to get greater realized returns from holding the lower-quality bonds?

As it turns out, we can. Realized returns do *tend* to become larger as you include lower-quality bonds in your portfolio. Again, you are earning an extra return as your compensation for taking a chance. In fact, realized returns are usually highest for the so-called junk bonds, or bonds issued by firms that are now in precarious financial positions. The returns are higher because the larger payments that actually are made more than make up for those that are missed. You win some and you lose some, but you usually come out ahead of the timid who stick with the bonds of AT&T.

However, as with the stock market, bond investors also earn nearly all of their risk premiums only in that special month, January.[4] Compute your monthly bond returns as we did for your stock holdings, and in all months—save one—you'll have a hard time telling the difference between the returns produced by junk and the returns produced by a riskless government bond.

Yes, Virginia, there *are* risk premiums.[5] But only in January.

MORE TAX ON THE BACK–END REQUIRES MORE RETURN ON THE FRONT–END

As an investor, the threat of the unexpected isn't your only concern. The IRS is eagerly waiting for a cut of your return as well.

It's no news that the IRS takes a bigger bite from some investments than from others. Invest in the bonds of states and local municipalities and they only take a bite of your capital gains. You keep all of your interest income (if you live in a state without an income tax). On the other hand, if you invest in corporate bonds, you're taxed on the interest as well.

Because the municipal is tax sheltered, you will probably prefer it to a corporate bond if both have the same default potential and the same yield to maturity. Consequently, if corporate bonds are to find a market, they have to sell at lower prices and promise higher yields to entice taxpayers to buy them and share their returns with the IRS.

In finance we call this extra return a *tax premium.*

Investments with greater tax exposure sell at lower prices and higher *pretax* expected return to make their *after-tax* returns comparable to tax-sheltered investments.

Incidentally, bonds aren't the only investments that the IRS treats differently. Some *common stocks* have greater tax exposure than others.

When you invest in a common stock, your return comes in two forms. As time goes by the stock can increase in price, and you get a capital gain. Prior to 1987, gains were taxed at a lower rate than ordinary income, and this was a definite advantage. However, capital gains have another advantage that still exists. You don't have to pay your capital gains tax until you realize, or cash in, the gain. You can keep the unrealized gain invested in the stock, and it will earn additional returns for you. It's sort of like getting an interest-free loan from the IRS. We all take interest-free loans when we can get them.

The other form of stock return is dividend income. Dividends are taxed right away, as received. No loan.

To minimize taxes, most of us would prefer to invest in stocks that emphasize capital gains over dividends. These are growth stocks that reinvest earnings back into the firm to enhance future profits. We don't get much in the way of dividends, but we do get tax-sheltered capital gains as the price of the stock rises with the market's expectation of higher future income.

The opposite of growth stocks are utility stocks. These don't reinvest most of their earnings. Instead, they pay them to investors now, as taxable dividends.

Invest in utility stocks, and you pay more taxes.

As with corporate bonds, you would expect a larger tax premium in the expected returns to utility stocks. Allowing for any differences in risk, utility stocks should have greater expected rates of return to compensate taxpayers for their greater tax exposure. Give me a higher rate of return on the front-end, because I've got to give more of my return to the IRS on the back-end.

The utility may have a smaller *risk premium*, but it should also have a larger tax premium.

Do stocks with greater tax exposure tend to produce greater returns on the front-end[6]? The evidence indicates that they do indeed. But again, the question becomes, "When?"

In January, that's when. In all other months of the year there's no discernable difference between the returns on high- and low-dividend paying stocks. Only in January do stocks with large dividends tend to have greater average returns than stocks with low dividends. In addition, the experts found something else that surprised everyone.

No dividends are completely different than *low* dividends.[7]

One study found the returns on *no*-dividend paying stocks to average 10 percent in the month of January. Ten percent in one month! The returns on *low*-dividend paying stocks averaged a respectable 2.5 percent in January, while the high-dividend paying stocks averaged about 5 percent. In the other 11 months, all stocks managed to produce a return of about 1 percent, irrespective of the size of their dividend.

So both risk premiums and tax premiums are, for the most part, earned within the confines of a single month. This comes as an astounding revelation to all those who have spent their lives studying and making money in the markets.

If you want nearly *all* the action, in terms of extra expected return that the stock market can provide, get in and out at the beginning and end of that single month. In all other months you might as well avoid risk-taking.

ENDNOTES

1. The Dow Jones Industrial Average is probably the most quoted market index, and the oldest. It was first published by Charles Dow in 1884 and included only 11 stocks. Since 1928 the index has included 30 companies. The Dow is not actually a value-weighted index; the weights of each stock are based on its price. But, because the index includes only very large companies, so-called blue chip, it behaves similarly to a value-weighted index.

2. The two returns will not significantly differ one from another. In general, because of the very high variability of stock prices, it is very difficult to establish statistical significance.

3. For a detailed discussion about the relationship between risk and return for various months, see Tinic and West (1984 and 1985).

4. See Chang and Pinegar (1986) and Smirlock (1985) for a discussion of returns in the bond market for different months.

5. In the month of January, there is a positive relationship between risk and return. However, we cannot conclude that risk alone can explain the high January returns.

6. The impact of dividends on stock prices is still an open issue. *In the absence of transaction costs* and other restrictions, most investors would hold stocks through the year except the four ex-dividend days. Corporations which are exempt from 80 percent of the dividends would collect all the dividends. In such an environment dividend yield does not matter. There is empirical evidence that indicates that investors do trade around ex-days (see Lakonishok and Vermaelen, 1983 and 1986). In addition, we expect to find that each corporation will attract to itself a "clientele" consisting of those preferring its particular dividend policy. The clientele effect was originally suggested by Miller and Modigliani (1961). Elton and Gruber (1970) attempted to measure the clientele effect by observing average price declines when a stock goes ex-dividend. Pettit (1977) and Lewellen, Stanley, Lease and Schlarbaum (1978) provide some empirical evidence supporting the clientele effect by examining accounts of individual investors handled by a brokerage house.

7. Companies that do not pay dividends tend to be small companies.

If We're So Smart . . . How Can The Market Be That Dumb?

This chapter is for those of you who are thinking, "There are plenty of really smart, money-loving people on Wall Street who'd just love to take advantage of something like the January Effect to make a fast buck. So why haven't they priced it away?"

That's a good question.

And it's really bothered most of the university professors who first stumbled onto the January problem. These are the guys who've held tenaciously to the belief that the stock market is capitalism in its purest form—Adam Smith's unbridled, invisible hand. If the system works well anywhere, it should work here. Competitive pressure should force stock prices to reflect the fair values of the firms that issue the shares. Prices in the stock market should reflect the stiff competition of millions of greedy investors, each trying to find a bargain before the other guy.

Imagine 10 million shoppers at a Bloomingdale's sale. How many real bargains are left after 10 minutes?

So why has the January Effect been around for such a long time?

If we all know that there are going to be some big returns in the market in January, we'll all want to buy stock on the day after New Year's Day.[1] But since the flood of orders will push stock prices up that day, we know we probably won't be able to get in at the bottom. As a result, some of us will get smart and buy before the market closes on New Year's Eve. Soon, as other people get smart as well, we'll see prices rising the morning of Dec. 31. So we'll begin to execute our trades on the day before. This, of course, may go on and on until the January Effect slides slowly into the preceding year and utterly disappears.

Has this happened? Will it happen? The answer depends on how efficient the stock market is at setting the right prices for stocks.

BEAT THE MARKET—IF YOU CAN

In a really efficient market you've got people scurrying around looking for bits and pieces of information that other people haven't heard about yet. There are lots of these people working really hard at this. Find something out *first* and try to make a fast buck. Every time they find something new, they either buy or sell stocks. The problem is that when they buy or sell they affect the price—slightly. With so many of them trying to make money, however, stock prices soon may reflect *everything* that's new. A piece of information may be news to *you* when you find it, but it's more than likely already reflected in the stock price.

Information already reflected in the stock price is worthless. And people have known this rather obvious fact for a long time. Take this statement by Richard Wykoff written in the *Magazine of Wall Street* more than 60 years ago.

> As far as news is concerned, there are two kinds: known and unknown. Known news is what we find on news slips, news tickers, and the usual run-of-the-mill letters. Known news is what has happened and has been told. It becomes public property the moment it is printed in Wall Street. *News known to everybody is, except in rare cases, of little use to anybody.*

True enough. But there's something else. The news that's reflected in stock prices doesn't have to be known to everybody. Many professional traders are both smart *and* powerful. Powerful in the sense that they control *lots* of money. If just a few of these traders find out something and buy or sell, they can drive the stock price to the point where it reflects what they know. At the extreme, once the market is truly efficient, prices reflect everything that is *knowable*. There's no way to consistently be the first to find out about what isn't presently knowable. So there's no way to consistently come out ahead of your competition.

You can't beat an efficient market. Unless perhaps you are an insider; and then you run an additional risk—jail.

SO HOW DO I TELL IF THE MARKET IS EFFICIENT?

Ten years ago most university professors thought the real stock market was very efficient.

They got that way from reading and writing hundreds of journal articles which tried to show that (a) stock prices respond quickly to events, (b) it's impossible for anyone to really beat the market, and (c) stock prices move randomly from day to day.

In this list *a* and *b* are obvious, but why *c*? Why should stock prices move randomly if the market is efficient? And what does it mean to move randomly, anyway?

To see what random is, let's think of something that isn't random. Throw a baseball at Reggie Jackson and let him blast one. Now let's examine the flight of the ball. The ball is going up, second by second. But each gain in altitude is smaller than the last. Finally it peaks out and begins falling. Each loss in altitude is now larger than the last. In any given second, the change in altitude for the next second can be predicted by looking at the preceding change. Not random.

When something is moving randomly, the next change can't be predicted at all by looking at the preceding changes. In 1905, in the scientific journal *Nature*, they called such a movement a "random walk." Suppose, they said, you leave a drunk in a field. Where should you look for him when you get back? If the drunk wanders around randomly, the best place to look first is right where you left him. The expected change in his position would be *no change*.

Similarly, if stock prices take a random walk, the best guess for tomorrow's price is today's price. The *expected* change in the stock price is *no change*. That's not to say that we don't expect the price to change. More likely than not it will move up or down by tomorrow. But, as with the drunk, we just can't predict the direction.

If the market is efficient, the next change in the price of any stock should be unpredictable.

Why?

In an efficient market stock prices supposedly reflect all knowable information. Think of the kind of information that is *unknowable*. First of all, it hasn't been received by anyone in the market. But more than that, it also must be impossible to predict that it's coming.

Unknowable information is utterly unpredictable; it flows into the market in a random pattern. Bits and pieces of previously unknowable information are coming in all the time, every minute of the day. Some pieces are relevant to a single stock—the main plant has burned down. But most affect the prospects for nearly all stocks—the Federal Reserve has changed its discount rate.

If efficient stock prices reflect all information, they must respond instantly to the receipt of new, previously unknowable information. And in responding instantly to each bit and piece of new information that randomly comes in, stock prices should themselves take a random walk. As simple as that.

In a way, it's ironic. Suppose that, at any point in time, Ford's stock price fully reflects the best possible forecast of all its future dividends using all available information and state-of-the-art analysis. Suppose, in addition, that GM's stock is being traded by people who have gone *completely* bonkers. These people haven't the vaguest idea what GM does, nor do they care. If you look at a history of prices for the two firms, you probably won't be able to tell which is which. Both will take a random walk.

If the people who trade GM *begin* to come to their senses, you may begin to detect some nonrandomness in the way the stock price changes from day to day. The price of GM may rise one day and get some of them excited about what might happen tomorrow. They will buy more of it the next day, and push it up further. Not random. The change that occurred today was caused by the change that occurred yesterday. As with Reggie's home run, the stock price now has *inertia*. At some point even these guys will realize the stock has been pushed too high, and they will start selling, driving it back down. Again, not random. The stock price is falling today *because* it went up too far yesterday.

Thus, it's only at the two extremes of complete chaos and total efficiency that we expect to see stock prices taking a random walk.

To sum this up we can say that, if the stock market is efficient, three things should be true:

1. Stock prices should react quickly to news.
2. No one should be able to really beat the market.
3. Stock prices should take a random walk.

Are these things true of the real market?
Let's see.

TELL ME: IS THIS MARKET EFFICIENCY?

It's pretty obvious that in an efficient market stock prices must react very quickly to news. How else could prices always reflect everything that is knowable?

Many of the first tests of stock market efficiency centered on the question: "How quickly do stock prices react to the announcement of important events?"

An important event is one that has a significant impact on the value of the stock. Most of the early studies of the speed of stock price reaction centered on events like takeovers, changes in the Federal Reserve discount rate, stock splits, and the reports of earnings-per-share.

The first problem faced by these studies was measuring the reaction of the stock price to the particular event. To measure this reaction, they looked at something we will call "extra return." In the course of a month, a week, or a day stocks produce monthly, weekly, or daily returns for their investors. Sometimes the returns are positive. Sometimes they are negative. In any case, you can come up with an estimate of what you would *expect* for the stock's return on any given month or day. The expected monthly return for a typical stock might be something like 1 percent. This is consistent with a 12 percent return for the year.

If, on a given day, a stock is reacting to an important event, its return for the day should be abnormal or atypical. It should be different from what you would normally expect.

Thus, the "extra return" for the month is the difference between the actual return and the expected normal return.

Suppose the event in question is something good. Something that should increase the value of the stock. In this case we would expect to see positive extra returns with the announcement of the event.

The question is, when will the extra returns come? On the day of the announcement? On the days before, as insiders get wind of what's coming? Or, on the other hand, on the days and even weeks *following* the announcement as the *inefficient* market gradually catches on to the significance of the event?

Nearly all the *early* studies of events showed that the reaction came at, or sometimes before, the time of the announcement.

Consistent with an efficient market.[2]

But . . .

These early studies had problems.

First, the market only reacts to unexpected events. If something happens exactly as expected, that's not news and the market's not going to react to it. Take a report of earnings per share for the year by

IBM. The market will react only if earnings turn out to be greater or less than expected. If greater, we expect positive extra returns on IBM; if less, we expect negative.

The early studies on earnings reaction usually classified firms into two groups: (1) earnings greater than expected and (2) earnings less than expected. They expected positive extra returns on the first group and negative on the second. The question was, when do the extra returns hit in relation to the time of the earnings announcement?

To learn this, you have to have a notion of what kind of earnings were expected, and this was part of the problem. The early studies often assumed something simple. For instance, they frequently assumed that earnings this year are always expected to be what they were last year. This is a simple rule, but it often doesn't work. If earnings are trending up, and *increase* in earnings may still be bad news if it happens to be below the trend.

With earnings expected to be growing at a 10 percent rate, if this year's earnings are $1.00, reported earnings of $1.05 (5 percent growth) next year would be bad news, not good.

A bad-news firm can easily be misclassified in the good-news group, blurring the results of the test. This bad-news firm may have negative "extra returns" *after* the announcement. These negative returns may help to cancel the positive extra returns occurring *after* the announcement for the other firms that have been correctly classified in the good-news group. It may look like there's little reaction after the announcement for the group as a whole.

But these naive notions of what the market *expects* from the event weren't the only problem of the early studies.

They usually looked at extra returns in terms of monthly periods. That is, they looked at the extra returns produced in the month of the event, the month before, the month after, and so on.

A month is too long a period to see what's really going on. If the event happens at the beginning of the month, and it takes the next 20 trading days for the market to fully react, a study looking at monthly extra returns will conclude the market is efficient. All the reaction takes place in the month of the announcement, and there will be no reaction in subsequent months.[3]

More recent studies have looked at *daily* returns, and also have come up with more reasonable notions of what the market expected to happen before the actual announcement.

The most comprehensive study on the reaction of stock prices to earnings reports was done by three professors named Rendleman, Jones, and Latane (1982).

To begin their study, they needed a measure of what the market expected the earnings for a company to be. By looking at the history of each company's earnings, they developed a statistical model which predicted the next quarter's earnings. They assumed this prediction was consistent with the market's expectation for what earnings per share was going to be announced.

Then they grouped firms on the basis of how far actual reported earnings deviated from this expectation. Companies with reported earnings *far* in excess of what was expected went into group number 10. On the other hand, firms with earnings far below what was expected went into group 1. With earnings slightly above or below expected, firms were in groups 6 and 5, respectively. Groups 9, 8, 7 and 4, 3, 2 were reserved for the intermediate cases.

If you invested in these groups 20 days before the earnings are actually announced, what kind of extra returns would you be earning as you approach and pass the announcement day?

The results of their test are shown in Figure 2–1. Day "0" is the day that the earnings were announced for all the firms. Keep in mind that this is a different *calendar* day for each firm. The extra returns for the different firms are aligned relative to the day earnings announced.

Let's look at group 10. Note the return accumulates to about 1 percent extra by the time we get to three days before the announcement. We then pick up an additional 3 percent extra in the next three days. The extra return comes from a ride up in the stock's price, and probably results from (a) insider trading just before the event and (b) the general market's reaction to the public announcement of the earnings report. By the way, the insider trading activity is illegal. So you're looking here at the tracks of many unconvicted felons.

From the issue of market efficiency, the interesting part is what happens *after* the announcement. Note that the extra returns *CONTINUE TO PILE UP FOR A FULL 90 TRADING DAYS!*

The stocks in group number 10 have nothing in common other than that they all reported surprisingly good earnings on day "0". Therefore, the continued pile-up of extra return for the group after the announcement is a delayed, and continuing, reaction to the

FIGURE 2-1

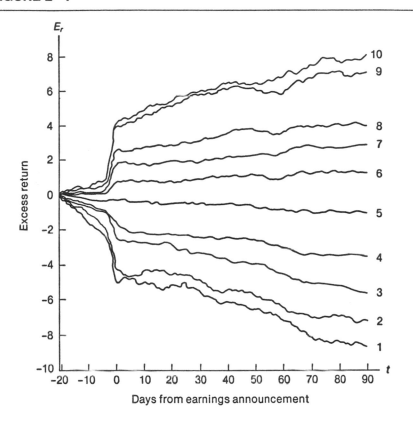

announcement itself. Where is the *instantaneous efficient market response?*

Now look at group 1.

The same thing is happening here in reverse. Negative extra returns continue to pile up for a long time after the announcement.

As we move from the extreme cases of 10 and 1, the tendency for extra returns to build after the announcement gradually disappears. Groups 5 and 6 show little or no tendency, because earnings turned out to be pretty much as expected for the firms in these groups.

Are these the tracks of an efficient market?

Hardly.

At this point the Rendleman study is the final word on the

efficiency of the stock market response to earnings announcements.[4] The time period and sample of companies studied here is very long and very large. In fact, it encompasses nearly all the time periods and samples of previous studies.

Is the stock market efficient in its response to the release of information about earnings?

The state-of-the-art answer to this question is . . .

No.

JOE GRANVILLE, HENRY KAUFMAN, OR BONZO. WHO SHOULD MANAGE *YOUR* STOCKS?

You can't beat an efficient market.

But Joe Granville, the famous chartist, says he can beat the market. Henry Kaufman, the guru of Salomon Brothers, says *he* can. If Ronald Reagan's friend Bonzo, the chimpanzee, could talk, we doubt if he'd have an opinion. But, if the market is efficient, each would have an equal chance.

If you are an efficient market devotee, and I ask you which of the three you want managing your money, your appropriate response should be, "Whoever is willing to work for less."

Bonzo will work for peanuts.

Would you really let Bonzo pick your stocks?

You might say, "Of course not! I've seen people come on Johnny Carson and other talk shows touting absolutely astounding records for picking stocks in the market. Joe Granville is one of them. I've read plenty of books by these kind of people, too. With track records like these running around, how am I supposed to think that everyone has an equal chance at beating the market?"

Don't dismiss the possibility just because you've come across people like Joe Granville.

Imagine that, someday, people become enamored with flipping coins. Not just *simply* flipping coins, but flipping them so that they come up "heads." Flipping "tails" is no good. "Heads" is the thing. Flipping "heads" becomes an art, then a science, and finally the national pastime.

Upon seeing this, TV magnate Ted Turner decides that it would be good for the welfare of the world if he organized the Coin Flipping

Olympic Games, to be held simultaneously in various stadiums all around the country.

Ted assures us that all coins used in the competition would be fair coins, so that the probability of getting a "head" on any given flip would be precisely 50 percent.

Well, this stirs the passions of dedicated coin flippers everywhere. Frenzied flippers make their way to their locally designated stadiums to begin the competition.

Since coin flipping, or more accurately "head" flipping, is now the national pastime, there are literally *millions* of competitors.

The competition begins—televised, of course!

In just 10 minutes it's all over. And some of the records are unbelievable!

Wow! People are emerging from the crowds with documented records of 25 heads in a row. Astounding! Publishers are after them to write books. Some of the best "head" flippers are scheduled to appear tomorrow on the "Today Show" and "Good Morning America." Everyone wants to know how they did it. How can anyone flip 25 heads without missing? That's harder than trying to pick the outcome of all the Super Bowls without missing one—or to pick 25 winning stocks in a row. How did they do it?

Luck.

With millions of people playing the game, records like that won't be common. But they definitely will exist, simply on the basis of pure chance. And you can be sure that the people behind them will tout their existence loud and strong.

But what about the tail flippers? There should be some astounding records at flipping tails, too. Why so many phenomenal "head" flippers and not a single "tail" flipper to be found:

> Losers
> hide.

It's the winners who shout and make themselves conspicuous. They write the books. They make the personal appearances. They collect from making the endorsements.

In the same way, even if the stock market is efficient, because so many people are playing the game, there should be plenty of market "phenoms" walking around bragging, writing books, and making personal appearances.

The question is, are there more of them than you would expect to see in an efficient market? And, are the people who are winning the types you would expect to win?

Who *would* you expect to win?

People who are smarter, better educated. The people who have more information. The people who spend more of their time trying to beat the market.

This description fits the *professional* investor. If the market is inefficient, professional traders should do *better* than amateurs. If the market is efficient, on the other hand, pro and amateur should be *indistinguishable* in terms of their market performance.

The professionals run the portfolios of mutual funds, insurance companies, banks, and pension funds. How have they done?

In 1969, Dr. Michael Jensen published the results of his Ph.D. dissertation completed at the University of Chicago. In it he examined the performance of professionally managed mutual funds. Jensen found that the mutual funds actually *underperformed* the market by about 1 percent per year. That is, you would have *expected* Bonzo to produce 1 percent more each year than the mutual funds did.

Perplexing indeed. Because it's just as hard to get beat by an efficient market as it is to beat one. It's just as hard to find an overvalued stock to buy as it is to buy an undervalued one.

So how did these mutual funds manage to turn the trick?

According to Jensen, they made a lot of fair investments *in* the markets but unfortunately, they made some really bad ones *outside* of the markets. For one thing, they hired professional security analysts who, according to Jensen, have little or no value in an efficient market.

Jensen proceeded to re-evaluate their performance after adding back to the returns all the "futile" expenditures made on analysts' salaries and other things like rent, data acquisition, and advertising for the fund. Lo and behold, after giving them back what they had spent foolishly, he found that the funds now *matched* the expected performance of Bonzo.

There are also more recent studies that show that professional portfolio managers do not outperform the market. For example, a study by Brinson, Hood, and Beebower (1986) reveals that pension fund managers during the period 1974 to 1983 achieved an average rate of return of 9.01 percent versus 11.11 percent for a benchmark portfolio. The performance of mutual funds in recent years is similar to that of the period examined by Jensen: at least two-thirds of the funds do not outperform the S&P 500.[5]

THE PLIGHT OF THE POOR PROFESSIONAL PORTFOLIO MANAGER

Jensen's initial study did much to fuel the fire of the efficient market and the ire of the professional manager. However, since its publication most of us have been persuaded that the measurement of the performance of portfolio managers is a more hazardous business than we initially thought.

For one thing, to say that you have *beat* the market means that we have to *define* what the market is. Is it the Dow Jones Average? The Standard and Poor's 500 Index? The New York Stock Exchange Index? Stocks and bonds? Or stocks, bonds, and real estate? What?

As it turns out, you can make your performance pretty much what you want it to be by changing what you mean by the market. Beat one index, like the Dow Jones average, get beat by another. On top of that, we just don't know which market index is *best* to use as a yardstick.

For another thing, a professionally managed portfolio is a constantly changing animal. If the pros think a bull market is on the horizon, they will move the portfolio to an aggressive posture. This means selling out of bonds and moving into the more speculative stocks that will respond vigorously to the bull market. If they think a bear market is coming, of course, they move in the opposite direction.

When you look at the returns on such a constantly changing portfolio, as Jensen did, you are really seeing a blurred, composite picture of performance of several different portfolios combined into one, all run by the same management team.

In a study that attacked this problem, two professors named Kon and Jen (1979) were able to separate the individual portfolio returns into two groups: (a) those coming from aggressive positions and (b) those coming from defensive positions. After separating, they saw a different picture than Jensen. They found some evidence that large numbers of these are professional investors who apparently can beat the market.

Who do you trust to pick *your* stocks?

Give Bonzo a banana, and let him sit this one out.

HARRY AND THE CHARTISTS

In the jargon of Wall Street, there are two basic types who try to make their living in the stock market: the fundamentalists and the chartists.

First, there are the fundamental analysts. These people look to what's happening outside their offices in the real world. They study the accounting statements released by firms. They watch the economy, consumer trends, shifts in the availability of resources. They try to figure out what these "fundamental" factors mean to the future earnings and dividends for the stocks they buy and sell.

Then there are the technical analysts.

Back in the 1950s a professor at the University of Chicago named Harry Roberts was amused by a growing band of stock market speculators who believed they could predict bull and bear markets by watching for patterns in the recent history of stock prices. These people called themselves technical analysts.

Chartists.

Seal most of these chartists in a room with no windows for their working day and, as long as they have air-conditioning, they won't care. What's going on outside isn't relevant, anyway. What does it matter if the unemployment rate doubled last month? Show them what happened to stock prices. That's all they care about.

They gaze intently at their funny-looking graphs. Some with bars and flags, some with X's and O's. They chart and wait. Wait for a sign. The signs usually look like *things*. A person, or at least the head and shoulders of a person. A person upside down. A flag. All sorts of funny things.

The things portend the market's future. If the person is standing right side up, that's bad. Upside down, that's good. How do they know? They've watched these things appear in the past and watched the market's reaction after their appearance. Events seemed to consistently repeat themselves.

Harry Roberts was definitely not a chartist, but as a highly trained statistician, he did pretty much the same thing chartists try to do. He tried to predict the future of something by analyzing the way it moved in the past. The difference between Harry and the chartists is that Harry's methods were scientific. Statistical analysis is based on a very carefully thought-out set of assumptions and mathematical proofs.

Rigorous.

Naturally, a statistician would be irritated by the heretics who thought they saw "flags" pointing the way to the future.

So Harry devised an experiment to clarify matters. In effect, he put little pieces of paper into a hat. Written on each piece was a dollar amount, each different. The dollar amounts represented *changes* in a stock market index, say the Dow Jones Industrial Average. Some of the changes were positive, and some were negative. The *average* value for the different changes written on the papers was 50 cents. And the extent to which the changes differed from piece to piece corresponded pretty much with the extent to which the Dow changed from week to week.

Then he started with a beginning level for his artificial stock market index roughly corresponding to the value for the Dow at the beginning of 1956, $444. He pulled a piece of paper from the hat that represented the change in the Dow for the first week. It read +$3. He adjusted the initial level by this amount, getting $447. He put the paper back into the hat, and pulled another out *at random*. After adjusting $447 by this second change, he continued for 50 more weeks. This artificial Dow was truly taking a random walk. Each successive change was unpredictable, having nothing to do with any of the changes that came before.

Now Harry asked the question, "Does this imposter look anything like the real McCoy?"

Let's see if *you* can tell the difference.

Take a look at the two charts in Figure 2–2 and 2–3. The 52 weeks of 1956 are running horizontally, and the weekly value for the Dow is plotted vertically.

Don't cheat by reading on. Which one do you think is real— Figure 2–2 or Figure 2–3?

Look carefully.

Will the real Dow Jones Industrial Average please stand up?

If you're like most people who've played this game, you picked Figure 2–2. Wrong choice. The real Dow is actually in Figure 2–3.

Most people are fooled by the head-and-shoulder pattern in Figure 2–2. That peak coming around week 30 is supposed to be the head of a person. If we are face to face, the smaller peak at 22 is the right shoulder, and the peak at 34 is the left. This person is not upside down, so this particular pattern bodes ill for the market. And, in this

FIGURE 2–2

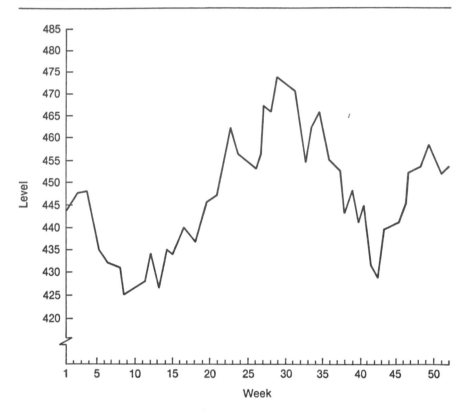

case, the signal turns out to be right, as the "Dow" continues to fall to $428.

Of course, this head-and-shoulder pattern had no forecasting power whatsoever. The changes that took us to $428 came from the same hat that produced the head-and-shoulder in the first place. All random draws. *Random.* But they produced a series that looks very much like the real stock market, including a classic pattern that sends chills down the spine of dedicated chartists everywhere.

Professor Roberts made his point. Many of the configurations chartists *think* they see are also present in a random walk.

Moreover, you apparently can't tell the difference between a random walk and the real stock market with the naked eye.

Okay, so they *look* alike. Does that mean they *are* alike?

No.

FIGURE 2-3

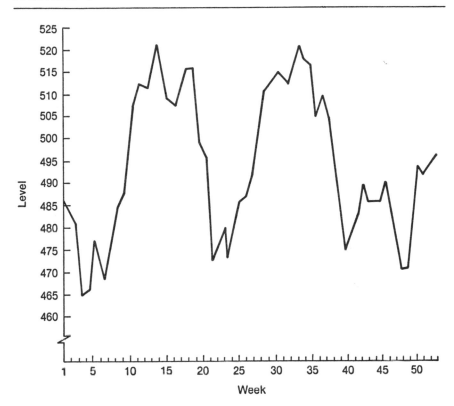

The naked eye is weak. At least when it comes to identifying a bona fide random walk.

So other professors began "looking" at stock prices with their powerful statistical microscopes. In the same year a fellow named Osborne (1959) and later people like Granger and Morgenstern (1963) and Fama (1965), reported tests supporting the randomness of the stock market.

The financial community wasn't amused. Especially the chartists.

A random market seemed to imply a senseless market. Like the one we talked of before, populated by people gone bonkers.

At least the fundamentalists found some solace. So long as they kept their investments firmly grounded in terms of projected earnings and dividends, they could wait out the random ups and downs of the "nuts" who traded short-term.

Then, however, Nobel laureate Paul Samuelson (1965) pointed to the other possible extreme. He showed that randomness may not be senselessness. Indeed, it could mean quite the opposite. If the stock market is completely efficient, and stock prices adjust to new information instantaneously, then stock prices will move in a random walk.

This revelation ruffled the feathers of the fundamentalists, who were previously unscathed by the efficient market theory.

And now there emerged a flurry of studies on the behavior of stock prices. From market averages to large numbers of individual stocks. From monthly changes in price to weekly, to daily, to trade by trade. From the New York Stock Exchange, to the over-the-counter markets, to the stock exchanges throughout the world. Never before had financial economists been in such a state of agreement.

Stock returns are *random*!

Not perfectly random, mind you, but random enough. Enough to be produced by an efficient market. Sure, a big increase in the stock price today increased *slightly* your expectation for tomorrow's change. But *only* slightly. So slightly that, if you paid commissions, you couldn't make any money from the market's little deviations from random behavior. Even the most avid advocate of market efficiency didn't expect *perfect* randomness, anyway.

The word was out. Stock prices follow a random walk, and the stock market is *efficient*!

There's no sense in doing technical or fundamental analysis to try to beat the market. An efficient market can't be beat by any kind of analysis. Want to build a stock portfolio? Hang the stock listings on the wall and throw darts at them.

Don't want to go to the trouble of picking stocks yourself? Hire a chimpanzee as your portfolio manager (Bonzo). He'll do at least as well as the pros. Maybe better. And he'll work for less.

Take two teams, one of professional portfolio managers and the other of civil engineers. One building a portfolio. The other building a bridge. Now have them switch jobs. You'd gladly invest in the engineers' portfolio, but we'll bet you wouldn't be caught dead standing on the bridge built by the portfolio managers. Intelligent people not only believed these things, the efficient market ideology fundamentally changed the nature of the game on Wall Street!

The mentality of efficient markets spawned the rise of indexed mutual funds. An index fund tries to match, rather than beat, a market index. Usually the Standard and Poor's 500. If the market is efficient, it can't be beat, even by the best of us. So why try? Instead of wasting your money futilely looking for under-valued stocks, indexed funds keep their staff and expenses down to a minimum. They promise to match the return produced by the 500 to within a percent.

By the end of the 1970s, a large fraction of money managed by mutual funds was invested passively by indexed mutual funds.

The efficient market was here—at least in the minds of professors and many practicing investment analysts. The case for the random walk had been accepted. But, as some were about to discover, it had also been very much overstated.

PARABLE OF THE PERPLEXED, POMPOUS PROFESSORS

In 1975, three professors at the University of Wisconsin were among the army of academics who had embraced the notion of an efficient market. Included in the three was one of the authors of this book. They were happy, because they had just signed a consulting contract with one of the major banks in Chicago to study the seasonality of interest rates.

It seemed that the bankers were absolutely sure there was a seasonal pattern in the interest rate on short-term U.S. Treasury bills. Now, they didn't want to bias the professors' study, so they didn't disclose what they thought the pattern was. Instead, they gave the professors a file of the daily interest rates on Treasury bills from 1955 through 1975 and sent them back to the ivory tower.

The professors took the data, and their consulting contract, back to Madison, Wisconsin, and happily stuffed the data into their computers with the statistical models, waiting to see a random walk come strolling out the other end. After all, Treasury bills are traded in a market very much like the stock market. They knew the stock market was efficient. The bill market should be efficient for many of the same reasons the stock market is.

So they tried to see if tomorrow's Treasury bill rate could be predicted by modeling the way the rate of today moved in accord with the rate of yesterday, the day before, and any number of other rates in days past.

As the results came churning out of their computers, they smiled knowingly. Treasury bills indeed followed a random walk.

Of course!

They knew that.

But they knew it wasn't going to be easy convincing the bankers of this. After all, the bankers had admitted to having preconceived notions. They probably saw all kinds of mirages in interest rates. Much like the head and shoulders that appeared in Harry Roberts' random walk. To convince them of the folly of their ways, the professors prepared a report of their statistical results, along with an extensive discussion of how easy it is to see funny things in numbers when, in reality, a trained statistician will tell you there's really nothing there at all.

The professors stuffed themselves into their compact car with their report and drove confidently down to Chicago.

Upon arriving, they were ushered into a large auditorium and onto a stage before 50 of 60 top executives in the bank. It took them 50 minutes to make their case.

Upon finishing, they looked up and smiled, ready to be congratulated and presented with their consulting fee.

Silence.

dead silence.

tick

tock

TICK

TOCK

It seemed to take a full five minutes before one particularly large and mean-looking banker broke in with, "I don't think you guys understand. We didn't hire you to come down here and tell us WHETHER there's a seasonal pattern in interest rates. We KNOW there's a seasonal pattern in interest rates. We just want you to MODEL the pattern. UNDERSTAND NOW?

Beads of perspiration began to form. What to say now? They don't believe us! They want more! But how do you model something you can't see in the first place?

"Look, professors. Maybe we can help you out. We didn't tell you what we thought the seasonal pattern was, because we didn't think YOU'D have any problem finding it, and because we thought if you knew about it in advance, it would BIAS your results. However, since you're having such a TOUGH time with this, maybe we'd better give you a CLUE. We think rates fall during the first month of the year, reach a trough in February, then rally, reaching a peak in August. From then on it's downhill again until February."

"Now, why don't you go back to Madison and take another look. When you're done and YOU see what WE see, let us know. We'll bring you back down. You give us the model and we'll write you a check."

It was a long drive back.

They spent the next two months twisting and turning the data this way and that. Maybe daily intervals are too short. Let's look at weekly Treasury bill rates. Monthly. Quarterly.

Nothing.

Then somebody suggested, "Why don't we line the rates up on the basis of the week of the year and then average them. You know, we'll take all the Treasury bill rates for the first week of the year for the entire 20-year period and find the average rate for the first week of the year. We'll do the same thing for the second week, the third, and so on."

Sounded like a good idea. So they produced the graph in Figure 2–4. Wow! There was the pattern.

Probably a fluke.

To prove to themselves that it was, they drew the same graph for only the even years, like 1962, and then only the odd years, like 1963. The pattern would probably disappear.

It didn't. The same pattern persisted in the graphs for both the even and the odd years.

Now the professors were beginning to think that something really *was* there.[6] But why couldn't they detect it with their statistical models? Back to the drawing board.

By this time they were convinced that, if they were going to capture the pattern with a statistical model, they would have to do it

FIGURE 2–4 Mean Weekly Returns

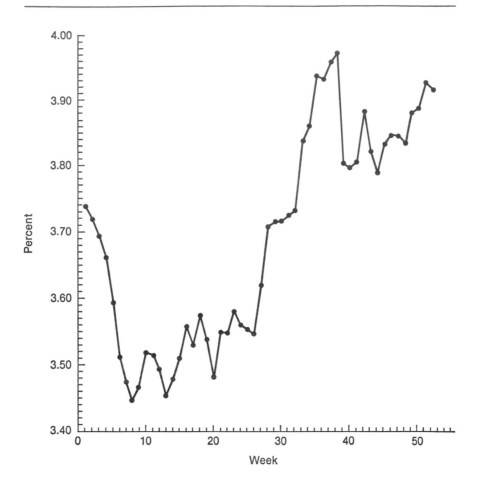

with quarterly data. But when they started the quarters at the beginning of January, April, July, and October, they still saw nothing but a random walk.

As a last resort, they began changing the beginning and ending weeks of each quarter. First, they started each quarter in the second week of the month, then the third, and so on. To their surprise, the computer results began changing dramatically.

Before, the computer was signalling random patterns. Now it was saying they were clearly systematic. The change that was occurring in the bill rate in one quarter could be related to changes in the rate that had occurred before. The series could be modeled!

The final result was a model that could predict the future direction of Treasury bill rates with 80 percent accuracy even when the predictions are made outside the period used to estimate the model.

Happily, the professors got their consulting check and something else, to boot.

They learned an important lesson. Take the most powerful statistical models known to man, casually pass them over a set of data, and you can easily conclude that the series takes a random walk. Even when important seasonal patterns actually exist. If you do not know where to look for something, you will probably not find it.

This had indeed happened time and time again. Not only in this little study, but quite possibly in the hundreds that preceded it allegedly documenting the so-called random character of stock prices.

It was the summer of 1975, and the January Effect in the stock market was about to be discovered.

A few hundred miles away.

ENDNOTES

1. Actually, to maximize the returns, an investor has to purchase the stocks on the trading day before the last trading day in December. Historically, high rates of return were observed on the last trading day of December, see Roll (1983) and Lakonishok and Smidt (1984).

2. A discussion of some of the earlier papers can be found in Copeland and Weston (1983) and Haugen (1986).

3. Monthly returns also have much greater variability than daily returns. This makes it more difficult to identify a statistically significant abnormal monthly return.

4. Givoly and Lakonishok (1979) found a delayed market response to revisions in EPS forecasts made by financial analysts. This is a similar result to the study of Rendelman, Jones and Latane (1982).

5. A recent study by Grinblatt and Titman (1986) examines the performance of mutual funds using various benchmarks.

6. In a recent paper, Park and Reinganum (1986) find puzzling behavior in Treasury bills that mature at the turn of the calendar month.

CHAPTER THREE

Tracks of a Giant

Eratosthenes is *not* a household word.

But Eratosthenes knew the world was round in the third century B.C., nearly 2,000 years before Columbus sailed his ships. He knew, because at noon on June 21, the longest day of the year, a perpendicular stick cast a shadow in his home town of Alexandria, but cast none in Siene, several hundred miles to the south.

This couldn't happen if the world was flat.

But he couldn't quite get his idea to catch on. So few of us have heard of Eratosthenes.

The glory goes, not to those who first discover, but to those who finally convince the rest of us that it's real.

Back in 1942 a fellow named Sidney Wachtel saw a year-end market effect, and wrote about it in an article published in an academic journal called the *Journal of Business*. In it he states,

> Tax-selling on the part of individuals and corporations operates on a calendar-year basis. Heavy sales toward the middle of December to establish tax losses tend to drive security prices below what they should be in the light of potential earnings. Following this hypothesis, the rise at year's end is nothing more than a normal reaction from depressed levels.

Aside from this tax-loss selling explanation, which was to be resurrected some 40 years later, Wachtel also alluded to a Christmas-related explanation.

> The unusual demand for cash, beginning a week or two before Christmas each year, causes many sales to be made "at market" on the security exchanges. Such sales also aid in driving down and ultimately bring about the reaction noted above.

Wachtel also speculated that a more select group of stocks than the Dow Jones Industrials could be compiled which would respond more readily to the stimulus.

As it turned out, this was an important conjecture. As discussed in the previous chapter, the reason the January Effect went undiscovered for so long is because it impacts predominantly on little companies. There are no little companies in the Dow and precious few in Standard and Poor's 500 Index.[1]

Figure 3−1 shows the average rate of return in January and the other months of the year for the Standard and Poor's 500 Index. Returns are computed by adding the change in the monthly value of the S&P to dividends paid to the stocks, then divide the capital gain and dividends by the value at the beginning of the month. The period covered is 1926 through 1985. While January's average return is relatively high, it certainly isn't unique. The months of July,

FIGURE 3−1   No January Effect for the S&P

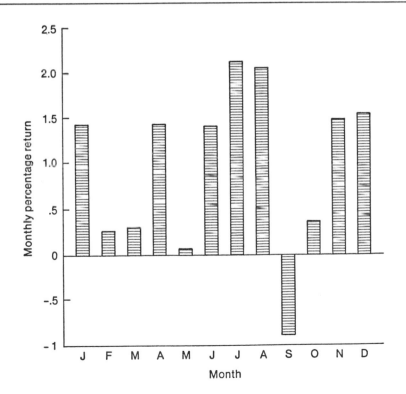

August, November and December, in fact, outstrip January's performance.

The January Effect simply can't be seen in the more closely watched market barometers.

So the effect went unnoticed.

There are some references in Barron's (August 5, 1940; December 2, 1940, and November 3, 1941) noting the unusual behavior of stock prices at the end of the year.

But a few sparks don't make a fire, and the idea went to sleep for a while.

For 35 years.

HAWKEYE

Let's begin this story with a place in space and time.

How about Iowa City, Iowa, and April 1975?

We're on the surprisingly pleasant and serene campus of the University of Iowa, standing in front of the not-so-pleasant-looking building housing the College of Business Administration.

If we walk up four floors we can reach the office of a new assistant professor named Mike Rozeff. Mike graduated with a Ph.D. from the University of Rochester last year, a student of Michael Jensen, one of the champions of market efficiency discussed in Chapter II.

As usual, Mike's door is open. He's going through some computer output showing the results of a pilot study.

Months earlier Mike's interest had been stirred by an article in the *Journal of Financial Economics* written by Robert Officer. Officer was looking for seasonality in stock prices in Australia. His results indicated something unusual going on in July, but Mike felt that, even if there was something there, you probably couldn't effectively pick it up using Officer's type of analysis.

Officer did something the three pompous professors initially tried to do. He tried to see if there was a relationship between the size of stock returns in a given month and the size of the returns in the previous month, the month before, and so on. If the return last month was unusually large, does that make us think the return this month will be unusual as well?

What if the thing that's unusual in that particular month, like July, for instance, is that it tends to have a big return?

Does that mean big returns in June will be associated with big returns in July?

No.

Does that mean *unusually* big July returns will be followed by *unusually* big July returns in the following year?

No.

You won't be able to spot the effect by correlating the returns in successive months, even if you leave gaps of various sizes between the monthly periods.

Although Rozeff is completely unaware of the comings and goings of his three pompous neighbors to the northeast, he's decided you have to do something similar to what they did in finding a seasonal pattern in Treasury bill rates.

Group the data by months of the year, and see if the average returns are significantly different.

He's done that, and now he's got the results. Results pertaining to an *equally* weighted index of stock returns. An index in which little companies have the same impact as big companies.

Listen.

"My Lord!"

He's just discovered the January Effect!

Mike promptly picks up the output and walks two doors down the hall to his friendly accountant, Bill Kinney. He and Bill had decided to look at January returns, because they thought January's *variance* would be higher due to the release of accounting information.

"Bill, what do you think of this? A seasonal in stock prices. Each one of these are average returns grouped by month. Look at this one. That's January!"

"You've *got* to be kidding, Mike! Is this *a* stock? For how long a period?"

"That's not *one* stock. That's *all the stocks* on the New York Stock Exchange, equally weighted. And it's going back to 1904. Before 1926 I used data from the S&P 500 Index and the Cowles Commission report on stock prices."

"Hard to believe. I thought you finance guys thought stock prices took a random walk."

"We did. We do. This doesn't show correlation, anyway. It just shows the return in January tends to be a lot higher than in any other month."

"But that January return is really big. It's *got* to be statistically significant. Probably economically significant, too. You could probably make money off it in the market!"

"Maybe so. In any case, it confirms my hunch that correlation studies will miss some forms of seasonality."

Rozeff picks up the output and turns to leave.

"Wait a minute, Mike. What are you gonna do with that, anyway?"

"Don't know.Probably file it and forget it. Why?"

"Look, I've been doing some work with this statistical technique called analysis of variance (ANOVA). It's a natural for this. Let's take a closer look at this thing and write a paper."

"Do you really think there's enough here for a paper?"

Yes, indeed!

What Rozeff and Kinney saw is presented in Figure 3−2. The

FIGURE 3−2 Results of Roseff-Kinney Study

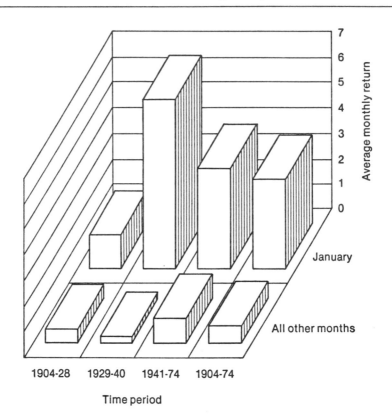

Average monthly return

January

All other months

1904-28   1929-40   1941-74   1904-74

Time period

bars in the back show the average rates of return for stocks on the New York Stock Exchange in January for three different time periods and the overall period, 1904 through 1974. As in the case for the S&P 500 graph, the returns include both capital gains and dividends. The bar to the extreme left partially reflects the returns for the Cowles Commission index, since Mike couldn't get NYSE data going back far enough. The other three bars, however, are representative of an equally-weighted portfolio of all NYSE stocks.

The index is equally weighted between the stocks. In other words, each index presumes you are investing an equal dollar amount of money in each stock at the beginning of each period. This means that we are looking at the simple average of the monthly rates of return for all the stocks represented in the index.

The bars in the front of the graph show the average rates of return for the other 11 months.

Remember, you're looking at *monthly* rates of return, not annual. For the entire period, January produces a rate of return that averages nearly 3.5 percent in a single month. If the rest of the months were like that, you'd be getting 50 percent per annum on your stock investments. But, as the front bars show, the other months produce a monthly return of only approximtely ½ of 1 percent.

Dividing the total period into sub-periods (1904 through 1928, 1929 through 1940, and 1941 through 1974) shows the January Effect isn't a product of one or two sensational Januaries. January dominates in each of the three periods.

Note that its dominance isn't as extreme in the early period (1904 through 1928). As we shall see in the next chapter, much of this period includes the period when capital gains weren't taxed (the income tax was instituted in 1917). Some believe that the January Effect is caused by tax loss selling of stocks at the end of the year. The relatively poor showing of January in the first period lends some support to this notion, although the early indexes used by Rozeff were value-weighted and therefore dominated by larger companies.

Another way to think about these results is to consider the fraction of a stockholder's total annual return that typically comes in January.

Figure 3-3, the pie chart on the next page, shows that, according to Rozeff-Kinney, *nearly one third of the total annual return for a typical stock comes from this single month*! That's, of course, about *four* times as much as you would expect.

FIGURE 3–3 January's Share of Annual Return: 1904–74

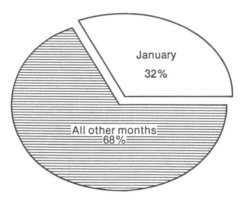

A THORN IN THE SIDE

This time around the issue didn't fall asleep. The reporting of a seasonal effect in the stock market in January stirred up much more excitement. Maybe it was because of the then-current embrace by the finance profession of a nearly religious belief in the concept of the efficient market.

Now there was new, exciting evidence of something clearly inefficient going on.

Another real irritant to the advocates of market efficiency appeared at the same time. This thorn was to inadvertently play an important role in the story of the January Effect. It was a paper published in the *Journal of Finance* by an accounting professor named Sanjoy Basu. Basu found that, if you bought stocks that had low ratios of price to earnings-per-share (P/E ratios), you could expect to beat the market averages, even after adjusting for the fact that your portfolio may have more or less risk than the market.

There's a good reason why this kind of strategy might work. But it's inconsistent with an efficient market.

A common stock investment, you see, is a different animal than a bond investment.

With a bond investment, your income is fixed at the level of the bond's interest payments. That's the most you're ever going to get.

But stocks pay dividends, and dividends are not fixed. They can get bigger.

They can *grow*.

Suppose you have two stocks that currently have the same earnings and dividends per share. For one of the two, earnings and dividends have been getting bigger. For the other, they have been getting smaller. Right now, they are the same.

For which stock should you pay more? The stock that has been growing, or the one that's been sliding?

That depends on whether the past says anything about the future.

Can you say that one stock is going to grow faster than another by looking at their track records?

Back before the 1920s, most professional traders thought the answer to this question was NO! Then, a security analyst's job was to come up with an accurate estimate of the *current* year's earnings per share. If *this* were a normal year for the company, what would we expect earnings to be? The stock would then be valued as a multiple of this normal earnings figure. The multiple was pretty much the same from stock to stock, changing maybe, with the risk of the stock.

The *future* growth of earnings and dividends wasn't even considered.

Why? Because they didn't think you could come up with reliable estimates of future growth.

Times changed in the '20s, when the *New Era Theory* came along.

In the '20s, *growth stocks* were the fad. The future is what counts! Buy the stocks today that will grow fastest tomorrow. Stock prices rose as growth stocks were bid up to extremely high multiples of current earnings.

Then came the crash and a reversion in the '30s to the old ways.

But growth stocks came back again in the '50s and '60s. Again, when you bought a stock today, you were paying in advance for *future* growth.

Which theory is right? Should we pay a higher price in advance for a stock we expect to grow? Can the future growth in earnings and dividends be forecasted with a reasonable degree of accuracy?[2]

The answer to this question seems to be, "Only for a very short time into the future." How far? Maybe 5 or 6 quarterly periods. Beyond that, the accuracy of statistical models and professional forecasts begins to fade so quickly that they are of little use.

But take a look at today's market.

Look at the differences in P/E ratios. Some stocks sell at prices that are only 4 or 5 times current income. Others sell at multiples of 40 or 50. Clearly, the market is betting that the 40 and 50 will grow faster for a *long* time into the future.

But, apparently you can't count on the future.

If this is true, you should stay away from the 50 and set your sights on the 4. The market may think this stock is in for a prolonged decline in earnings, but you can't count on that, either.

It's probable that the 4 will not do much worse than the 50 in terms of future earnings growth, and, if that's the case, the market will bid the price up as soon as it discovers its mistake.

Therefore, low-P/E stocks may produce higher rates of return for their investors.

Many before Basu had tried to show this same thing by back-testing the strategy with past returns. Proponents of market efficiency were quick to point out the fatal flaws in these studies, however.

One flaw, particularly fatal and particularly common, was the way these people picked groups of firms to study. Suppose they were going to examine the performance of low-P/E stocks during the 1970s. Typically, they would look at a group of stocks, all of which were in existence both at the beginning and the end of the period.

The problem with this is that you automatically avoid the real threat you've always got to worry about with a low-P/E strategy. Let's face it. You're purposely investing in the "dogs" of the market. The market thinks the future of these companies is bleak. That's why the price is low in relation to earnings. The market thinks that the company behind the stock may be in trouble. Bankruptcy and liquidation may be around the corner.

The market could be right. And, if the firm goes bankrupt, the return on your investment in its common stock is likely to be *minus* 100 percent.

However, if in testing a low P/E strategy, you pre-screen your sample of stocks to ensure that they will all pass through the test period unscathed, you don't have to worry about the bankruptcy problem.

Okay, so your P/E study shows high returns. What does that mean to me, a poor investor, who's not omniscient, and who must face the threat of bankruptcy? After all, *I'm* the one who has to put my money on the line by investing in a bunch of stocks the market thinks has a good chance of going under.

The advocates of the efficient market gleefully shot down these studies by pointing out this fatal flaw.

Then along came Basu.

He constructed his sample by selecting stocks at random at the beginning of his study period. No effort was made to ensure that any of these firms would actually survive for the duration of the period. He classified the firms into five groups according to their P/E ratios at the beginning of each year. He then measured the performance of each of the groups during the period April 1957 through March 1972.

Basu's results are shown on Figure 3−4 below. Let's first look at the columns at the rear of the graph. These show the average annual rates of return (including both dividends and capital gains) to each of

FIGURE 3−4 Low P/E: High Return

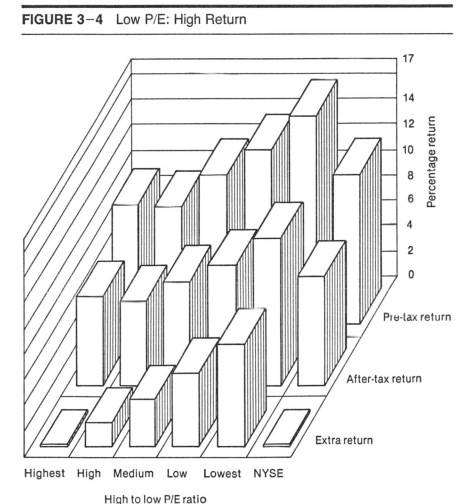

the five groups and to the New York Stock Exchange Index. Notice that the returns are lowest for the high-P/E group and highest for the low-P/E group. The NYSE index comes in about in the middle.

During the period of this study, capital gains and dividends were taxed at different rates. To see if this has any impact on the results, Basu computed after-tax returns, assuming you are in the 50 percent bracket and capital gains are taxed at 25 percent. These after-tax returns are shown in the middle row. Pretty much the same pattern.

Maybe the low P/E group has more risk, and the difference in return is just a risk premium to compensate you for taking the greater risk.

Basu's results, however, show that the low-P/E group actually has somewhat *lower* risk than its high-P/E counterparts. The bars in the front row of the graph show the extra return on the high-, medium-, low-, and lowest-P/E groups in comparison to the return produced by the highest-P/E group after allowing for risk. Notice that as P/E goes down, the extra return becomes larger and larger.

But wait a minute. If I keep rolling my portfolio over to get into low-P/E stocks, I'm going to burn up a lot of bucks in commissions. Are these differences in returns large enough to compensate for this and still give me a meaningful edge in my performance?

Yes.

Okay, so there are still differences in the returns, but are they large enough to be statistically significant after allowing for the variations in the returns from year to year? Maybe these differences are due to chance.

As a matter of fact, there is less than a 1 percent chance that these differences in performances are attributable to Lady Luck. The odds are overwhelming that something other than chance is at work here.[3]

Market inefficiency?

This study was a real problem for the high priests of market efficiency. These results were *pretty* hard to debunk!

Speaking of high priests, every religion has its holy place. Jerusalem . . . Mecca . . .

So now our story turns to the Great Temple at the Holy Place of Market Efficiency. The Graduate School of Business at the University of Chicago.

LITTLE STOCK BIG RETURN

What to do about Basu?

You just can't beat the market by investing in low-P/E stocks. We know that.

Basu's results must somehow be consistent with the efficient market. It's simply a matter of finding out how.

Around the time of the publication of Basu's results, the University of Chicago set out to find the source of the Basu anomaly.

Aha! It's as simple as this.

The companies of stocks that have low P/Es also tend to be small themselves. Take Figure 3−5, which is from a later study by Basu (1983). It's pretty obvious that the stocks with the lowest P/Es also are the smallest in terms of the total market value of their common stock (the number of shares outstanding multiplied by the market value of each share).

FIGURE 3−5 Little Companies Have Low P/E Ratios

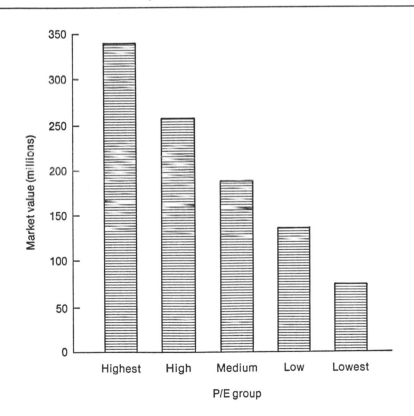

Now think about investing in little companies. In the first place, it costs more to trade in the shares of small companies. The market makers for different stocks on the New York Stock Exchange, American Stock Exchange, and Over-the-Counter markets know that the shares of little companies trade less frequently. Because of this they charge a higher margin on their trades in the stock. That is, if you want to buy shares of a little company from them, they will ask a price that is considerably higher than the price they bought the shares for. It's like with any other product. If your volume of sales is lower, you've got to make more on each sale to make a decent buck.

Brokerage commissions are also structured so that you pay a higher percent commission of trades in low-priced than in high-priced shares. It also turns out that the shares of little companies tend to trade at lower prices than big ones.

In the second place, there's a risk factor separating big from little companies. Big companies tend to release more information, and they are more closely watched by not only the news services, but the investment industry. More is known about big companies than about little companies. This adds a certain dimension to the risk of investments in small stocks that might not have been captured by Basu's risk adjustments. Basu just looked at the volatility in the stock price. He didn't look at how *much* investors knew about the companies behind the stocks.

Because of the additional costs of trading and the additional risks of trading in small companies, investors may demand a higher expected return on them. If they do, we shouldn't be surprised to see small companies producing bigger returns.

Again, small companies tend to have low P/E ratios.

So low-P/E stocks should produce big returns as well.

Even in the efficient market.

Basu wasn't seeing a P/E effect. He was seeing the small-firm effect in disguise. A P/E effect, standing on its own, *is* inconsistent with market efficiency. But if stocks with low P/Es tend to produce high returns just because they also tend to be small companies . . . . then there's nothing wrong with this. Small companies are riskier. They cost more to trade. They deserve to have higher returns.

Chicago dissertations by Rolf Banz and Mark Reinganum revealed the actual presence of a size effect in stock returns. They showed that if you first classify stocks by size and then, within each size grouping, classify again by P/E, you will find that the low-P/E stocks don't have higher returns than the high-P/E stocks *of the same size grouping*.

Now, Basu didn't take this lying down.

He came back with Figure 3−6.

Going across the rows from left to right, we move from the smallest *size* group to the largest. Within each size group, as we move toward the back of the chart, we move from the stocks with the highest P/Es to the lowest.

There seems to be both a size effect *and* a P/E effect.[4]

FIGURE 3−6   Size or P/E Effect?

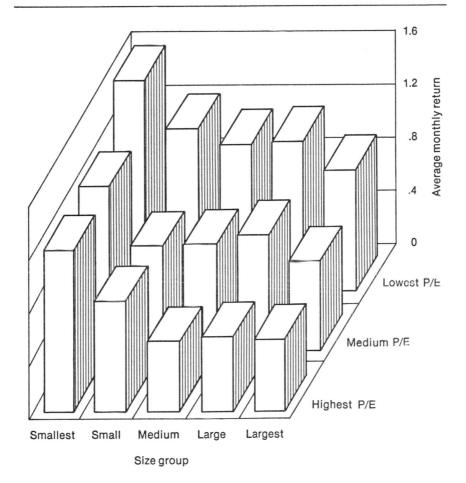

Look carefully at the bars showing the average monthly returns to the smallest companies. See the big jump in returns as you go from small to smallest?

A later, more detailed study of the size effect by Donald Keim (1983) showed the size effect isn't quite as simple as first imagined.

Take a look at Figure 3–7.

In this study, Keim ranks firms by the total market value of their stock. He then measures the extra returns (the difference between what they actually produce and what they should, given their risk) and finds the pattern depicted in the graph.

The small-firm effect really begins to intensify as you get into companies with less than $200 million in total stock outstanding.

The smallest firms tend to produce tremendous returns for their investors.

FIGURE 3–7 Keim: Small Firm Effect

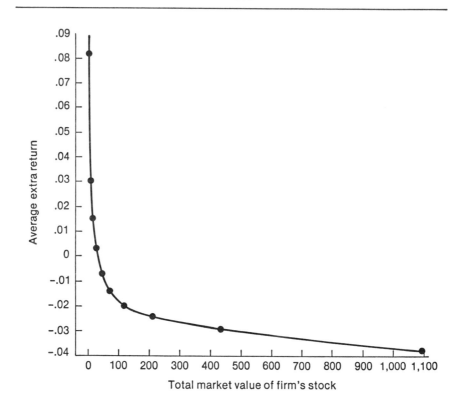

Do you know any really successful investment managers?

Ask them if they invest in small firms.

Now, a small-firm effect, even of this size and shape, is still perfectly consistent with market efficiency because size may be serving as a proxy for risk. So, even though the P/E effect could not be completely ruled out, the advocates of market efficiency were still comforted by the fact that part of it could be attributed to the small-firm effect.

At least, until they found out that nearly all the premium for investing in small firms was earned in a *single* month.

LITTLE STOCK BIG JANUARY

And so it was written.

"There *is* a size effect in stock returns."

Having been blessed by the Holy Temple as a topic worthy of scientific investigation, hundreds of tenure-seeking assistant professors, among others, trained their sights on the size effect.

Fortunately for them, the rates of return for all stocks on the New York and American stock exchanges had previously been painstakingly and accurately recorded in the Temple, and then sold on computerized tape to the research universities around the world.

The computers started spinning from California to Tel Aviv.

The *Journal of Financial Economics*, one of the leading journals in the field, decided to devote an entire special issue to the topic in 1983. The issue was called "A Symposium on Size and Stock Returns and Other Empirical Regularities", and it contained eight papers devoted to the size effect and the January Effect.

Why the January Effect? Because, as it turns out, the size effect basically comes in January.

One of the papers in the special issue was written by Donald Keim from the Wharton School at the University of Pennsylvania (based on his dissertation completed at the University of Chicago). We've already seen a graph from this particular study. Go back and look at Figure 3–7. Each one of those dots is a group of firms. As you move from left to right, you're going from the smallest firms to the largest firms.

Now look at the difference between the extra return (what you're getting beyond what you'd expect, given their risk) to the smallest firms (.082 percent per day) and the return to the largest firms (−.038

percent per day). The total, annual *difference* in the extra return is .082 percent less −.038 percent, or .12 percent per day.

Figure 3−8, Difference: Extra Return on the Smallest and Biggest, is also from the Keim study. It shows the monthly average of the daily difference in the extra return earned by the small and the large in each January from 1963 to 1979. Small firms consistently produce bigger returns than large firms.

Keep in mind that Keim has adjusted for the fact that the small firms are riskier, in the sense that their stock prices are more volatile. Even after allowing for an appropriate risk premium in their returns, small firms consistently produce a larger return.

But *when* during the year is this total annual difference in the extra return to small and big companies earned?

Figure 3−9 provides the answer.

FIGURE 3−8   Difference: Extra Return on Smallest and Biggest

---

FIGURE 3-9 Annual Extra Difference by Trading Day

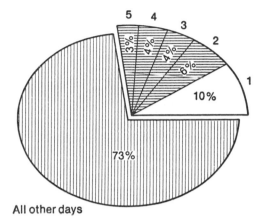

All other days

The lion's share of the small-firm effect comes in January. As a matter of fact, it's the first five trading days in January that really stand out.

Small firms earn nearly an additional 4 percent more on the *first* trading day. Quite a head start for the rest of the year!

More than a quarter of the small-firm effect is earned in the first trading week of the year.[5]

What kind of an efficient market is *this*?

WE ARE THE WORLD

It's August of 1983 and Gultekins are making tracks for Madison, Wisconsin.

Gultekins???

The Brothers Gultekin!

Bülent and Mustafa.

Their work (1983) is about to be presented at the first Johnson Symposium in Finance at the University of Wisconsin.

The brothers came to the United States from Turkey. Bülent is an assistant professor at the Wharton School of Finance and Mustafa is working toward a Ph.D. at New York University. These guys are among the army of young academics inspired by the growing excitement and controversy surrounding the January Effect.

Actually, *both* of them aren't physically going to Madison. Only Bülent. But he's carrying their joint work—work that will blow the January controversy wide open.

You see, being from Turkey, they have an interest in things international. With everyone running around screaming and yelling about the January effect, they decided to check out whether it was a local phenomenon.

So they applied the Rozeff and Kinney technique to 16 foreign countries with stock markets. Why not? Who knows what they'd turn up?

For each country they gathered prices on stock market indexes (like the New York Stock Exchange Index for the U.S. market). Then they computed the monthly percentage changes in the indexes and categorized them by month. Dividend income is not reflected in the percentage changes. The time period they looked at was the months including and between January 1959 and December 1979. The countries they looked at included:

1. Australia	9. Japan
2. Austria	10. Netherlands
3. Belgium	11. Norway
4. Canada	12. Singapore
5. Denmark	13. Spain
6. France	14. Sweden
7. Germany	15. Switzerland
8. Italy	16. United Kingdom

What was the average percentage change in January? And how do these changes compare with the rest of the months of the year?

The astonishing answer is revealed in Figure 3–10.

Wow!

Incredible! The January Effect is nearly everywhere! And the January returns are huge! Even bigger than in the U.S.

Now, for the first time, we can begin to come to grips with the scope of the force we are dealing with.

Take a long, close look at Figure 3–10. Consider carefully what you are seeing.

You're looking at the tracks of a GIANT.

A force of momentous proportions. A force that can increase the market value of firms all over the world by 3.5 percent on average in a

FIGURE 3–10 International January Effect

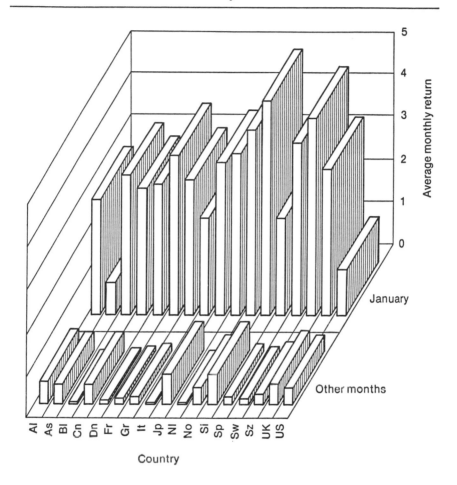

single month. And the giant returns again year after year. His foot-prints are measured in *trillions* of dollars!

Here are some of the startling facts behind that graph.

1. January is the only month of the year with a positive return for every country.
2. In 65 percent of the countries, January contributes more than 50 percent of the total return for the year (excluding dividends).

3. In Belgium, the Netherlands, and Italy, the average return in January is greater than the average return for the whole year. This means that the average return for the other 11 months has actually been negative in these countries!

Amazingly, January has been even more exciting in other countries than in the United States.

These results had a profound effect on the profession. The domestic results were not a fluke. They could not be dismissed as an aberration attributable to some idiosyncracy in the United States financial system. We were dealing with something really big. Something immensely powerful. Something of global importance.

But what?

Publication of the Gultekins' results stimulated others to conduct more detailed examinations of what was happening in January in the international stock markets.

Immediately, researchers began finding the size effect on an international scale. In Finland, the United Kingdom, and Canada, little companies were again shown to be producing extra returns above and beyond what could be justified on the basis of their risk.

Then a professor named Kiyoshi Kato from Nanzan University in Japan teamed up with Jim Schallheim, a U.S. professor, to see what was going on in January on the Tokyo Stock Exchange. They looked at the returns on stocks from 1964 through 1981. Their sample starts with 529 stocks in 1964, and it gradually increases to 844 stocks in 1981.

At the beginning of each year, the two professors ranked all the stocks in their sample by the total market values (number of shares times price per share) of their outstanding common stock. On the basis of this ranking, they then split the stocks into 10 groups, from the largest to the smallest.

For each group, what were the average returns in January and in the rest of the months of the year?

Look for the answer in Figure 3−11. The results shown in the chart are strikingly similar to those found by Keim in the United States. The small-firm effect in Japan is also concentrated in the first month of the year.

In case you have begun to speculate on a possible cause for all this, and looking ahead to our later discussions in Chapter IV, you may want to note something right now.

There is no tax on capital gains in Japan!

FIGURE 3–11 January-Small Firm Effect in Japan

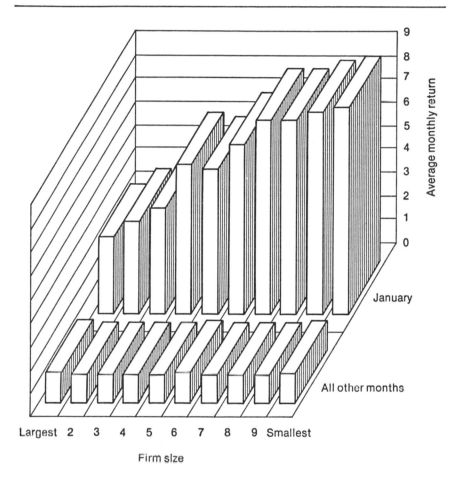

WHEN DO *YOU* CORRECT *YOUR* MISTAKES?

The plotter just ran out of ink.

"Blast it!"

Werner De Bondt shrugged off one more frustration and quickly made his way to the supply room to find one of the special pens required by the computerized plotter. This had been a long, *long* day, beginning at about six this morning.

It is now 6 P.M., and we are in the summer of 1984 in Ithaca, New York.

The young man from Belgium is completing work on his Ph.D. dissertation at Cornell University. Werner is writing under a professor named Richard Thaler, a behavioral economist.

A behavioral economist won't have much sympathy for the University of Chicago's view of the efficient stock market. In finance, behavioralists are part of a new, emerging school of thought.

The more traditional theories in finance are founded on the assumption that all human beings behave in a perfectly rational manner. Now, this is obviously not true in general. You've probably seen as many nutty people wandering around the streets as we have.

But it's a pretty reasonable assumption to make about the stock market. Why? Because, *if* stock market prices weren't set in a rational manner, smart, rational people could think of ways to make all the money they want by taking advantage of their less rational counterparts.

So most of us in finance think it's okay to assume that stock prices are set *as though* everyone playing the game were as emotionless as Darth Vader and as smart as Albert Einstein.

The new, emerging school doesn't buy this.

They think that emotions work their way into stock prices. All kinds of emotions. Panic. Depression. Zeal!

De Bondt and Thaler, in particular, feel that investors in the stock market tend to overreact to things. Good news gets blown out of proportion, sending stock prices to inflated levels. Bad news pushes the stock market into deep depression, driving stocks dirt cheap.

As we said before, when the market gets irrational, there's money to be made. And, if you believe De Bondt and Thaler, the way to make money is to buy the stocks that have performed poorest in the past and avoid the super performers as though they had the plague.[6]

A test of this hypothesis is the subject of Werner's dissertation.

To see if it's true, he and Thaler looked at thousands of common stocks listed on the New York Stock Exchange. They then computed the returns for these stocks in all possible annual overlapping five-year periods from 1926 to the most recent period of available data. Within each five-year period they ranked the stocks by their return for the period. They were interested in the stocks that had done extremely well and extremely poorly. So they separated the top and bottom 50 stocks in the rankings for each period.

They have a prediction for the performance of these "winners" and "losers" in the periods following the performance evaluation and ranking. The stocks in the winning group had obviously been the beneficiaries of good news in the five-year period. The market drove the prices of these stocks up. Up too far, think De Bondt and Thaler. The market overreacted, as it usually does. The opposite, they think, has happened to the losing stocks.

If this is true, the overreaction is likely to be followed by a correction. In the next five-year period the relative performance should reverse. The stocks in the winning group should under-perform the market at the same time that the stocks in the losing group are beating the market.

So Werner computed the difference between the average of the returns for each group and the return for the New York Stock Exchange Index. If they are right, in the next period, the losers should produce returns that are greater than the index, while the winners should get beaten by the index.

Werner has spent this day, and the days of the past several weeks, computing the differences in the returns and then averaging them over the overlapping five-year test periods.

Each five-year test period ends in December.

The pen has been replaced, and the computer begins to plot.

We'll concentrate on the losing group first, and begin with the first month of the plot. This first month is the first January following each of the first five-year periods. Take each of the stocks in the losing groups in each of the periods. Now compute the difference between *their* rates of return in the next January and the return for the *market index.* Do this for all of the overlapping test periods, and then average the differences.

Plot this average difference for month "1" on the graph.

Then we move on to February. The same difference between the losers and the market is calculated and averaged. February's average difference is added to January's, the total is plotted, and we move on to March.

The plotted line is moving up, showing that the losers are produc-ing bigger returns than the market.

De Bondt and Thaler are getting the result they expected.

But what's this? The line for the losers *is* rising, but it's rising in a series of *steps.* For 11 months it stays almost flat. And then it jumps up.

And it jumps only in January.

The plot is finished, and you can see it in Figure 3–12.

Again, take a long, close look at this truly astounding plot.

The previous losers rise, producing returns higher than the market's, and the previous winners fall, producing returns less than the market's. A correction of the overreaction in the previous five years. But if you look closely, you can see that the corrections come only in January. Notice that the corrections gradually become smaller and smaller. But, at least in the case of the losers, you can easily pick out the Januarys in the plot even as far as five years out. This is five years after the losers were assembled as a group. They are still moving up. And they move only in January.

If what we are seeing is truly a correction of a past mistake, the market corrects its mistakes only in January.

Why?

Notice also that the winners tend to rise slightly in November and December, just before their fall in January.

On the days and weeks that followed, Werner and Dick confirmed these results by measuring performance in many different ways, including adjusting the returns for the relative risk of the

---

FIGURE 3–12

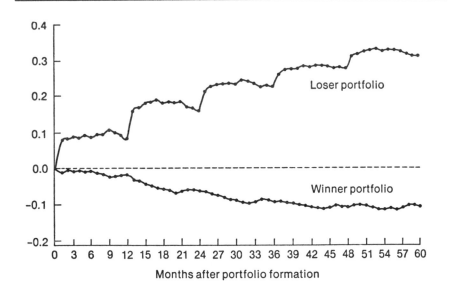

Months after portfolio formation

winning and losing stocks. The results all turned out pretty much the same.[7]

But the corrections still came in steps. And you climbed the steps in January.

The market corrects its mistakes in January.

Why?

WHEN RISK EARNS ITS REWARD

Back to the Temple.

Written on the scrolls in the Temple was a theory about risk and expected rates of returns on financial investments. The theory was called the Capital Asset Pricing Model, and it was revered by the high priests of market efficiency.

The basic idea behind the theory is that investors worry about variability in the returns to their *portfolios* of investments. When they look at an individual investment, like a stock, they ask, "If I add this to my portfolio, how will it affect the stability of the portfolio's periodic returns?"

What will be the contribution of the stock to the risk of your total portfolio?

As it turns out, you can measure this contribution by something called *beta*.

So what is beta?

Beta tells you the extent the stock moves up and down with the market. Suppose a stock has a beta of one half. This means that if there is a change in market return of 1 percent you would expect a change in the stock return of one half of that, or 5 percent. If, instead, the stock had a beta of 1.5, you would expect the change in its return to be 1.5 percent. The bigger the beta, the more responsive the stock to movements in the market. Stocks usually range in beta from 0 to 2. Public utility stocks usually have little betas and airline companies usually have big betas.

The bigger the beta, the bigger the risk.

In the capital asset pricing model, the return you can expect to get on a stock can be divided into two parts.

The first part is the risk-free rate. This is the rate of return you can get on a riskless security, like a U.S. Treasury Bill. If you invest in a common stock, you're going to at least want this.

The second part is a risk premium—an additional increment in expected return to compensate you for investing in a security as risky as a stock.

Now the size of the risk premium for any stock is related to the size of the stock's beta. The bigger the beta, the bigger the risk—and the bigger the beta, the bigger the risk *premium*.

A typical, run-of-the-mill stock will have a beta equal to 1. A stock like this is supposed to carry an average risk premium (This will be the risk premium attached to the market as a whole. What if you invested in all the stocks in the market? What would you expect in return beyond the Treasury Bond? This is the market's expected risk premium, and this is the risk premium you expect with a stock with beta equal to 1.)

A stock with twice the average risk will carry a beta of 2. The risk premium for this stock will be twice as large as the market's. Similarly, with a beta of .5, the risk premium will be half the size.

What could be more fair? If you're willing to take on some risk, you can *expect* to earn a reward based on the amount of risk you take.

Of course, things may not turn out as expected. Airline stocks sometimes produce really awful rates of return. But that's part of taking the risks. You're not guaranteed a higher return.

Nevertheless, you *expect* to get one.

But *when* do you expect to get one?

It would seem reasonable that, if you invest in an airline stock in May, June, July, or August, you should *expect* to get a risk premium. After all, Frontier Airlines went bankrupt in August. You're at risk throughout the year. You should be compensated for this risk throughout the year.

This idea of earning a risk premium is a basic tenet of finance. It's on all the scrolls in the temple—at least, nearly every one.

The professors of finance spend much of their time observing and tracking the performance of the market, trying to measure the risk premium in its expected rate of return. To their satisfaction, they have found that there *is* a risk premium in the market's expected rate of return.

The evidence supported the theory of the scrolls, and there was peace in the kingdom.

At least until Seha Tinic, a professor from the University of Texas, and Richard West, the dean of the Graduate School of Business at New York University, noticed something funny.

The stocks with the biggest betas tended to produce the biggest returns for their investors only in one month of the year.

January.

In the other months, you couldn't expect high-risk stocks to produce higher than average rates of return. Their expected returns were pretty much the same as on low-risk stocks.

Only in January, when returns overall tended to be very large, did the stocks with big betas tend to produce the highest rates of return.

Only in January did the market deliver its promised risk premium to its investors.[8]

Tinic and West looked at monthly risk premiums to all the stocks on the New York Stock Exchange in ther period 1935 through 1982. After separating by month of the year, they found the results (1985) presented in Figure 3−13.

In the graph we've got four set of bars, each for a different time period. Let's concentrate on the most recent period, 1969 through 1982.

In an average January for the period, the market delivered a risk premium of about 6 percent—that is, if you could expect to get a *monthly* rate of return of 2 percent from a zero beta stock, you could expect a *monthly* 8 percent return from a typical stock.

That's a lot of compensation for bearing some risk for a single month.

But what about the other 11 months? You get nothing. The risk premium is virtually *zero*. On the average, airline stocks produced the same type of returns as utilities.

And basically, the same is true for all the other periods they looked at.

Common stocks are risky investments throughout the year, but your compensation for bearing that risk comes only in January.

Another crack was developing in the foundation of the temple.

And now attention quickly turned to the bond market. When do bonds earn *their* risk premiums?

This question was answered by Donald Keim and Robert Stambaugh, a professor at the University of Chicago. They looked at the risk premiums on bonds during the period 1926 through 1978. The risk premiums were the differences between the returns produced by the bonds in each month and the returns produced by riskless government securities. Again, they categorized their results by month of the

FIGURE 3–13 Risk Premium in Stock Market

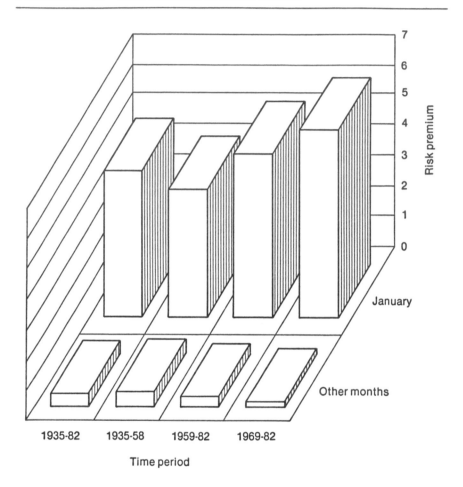

year, and they grouped their bonds into three classes; high grade, medium grade, and low grade. The high-grade bonds are rated above Baa by Moody's investment service. Medium-grade are Baa-rated. And the low-grade bonds are rated under Baa.

Their results are presented in Figure 3–14.

Again, the low-grade bonds produce bigger returns than the high-grade only in January. In the other months of the year you might as well keep your money in Treasury securities. You can expect to get the same return there as you can expect in corporate bonds. And remember—the Treasury can print money to pay off its bonds. General Motors can't.

FIGURE 3–14 Risk Premium in Bond Markets

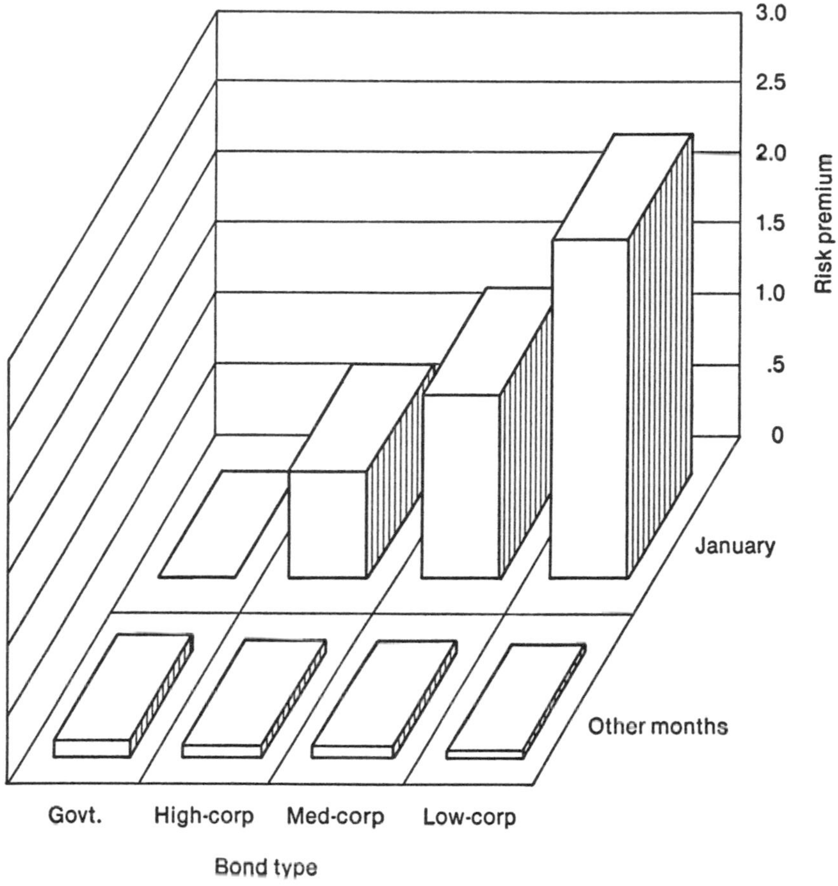

Both stocks and bonds deliver their risk premiums in a single month.

Why?

And what to do with all these scrolls?

AND NOW, THE TAX PREMIUM

We all know that municipal bonds have lower returns than corporate bonds because their investment income is largely tax-exempt. Their lower pre-tax return makes their after-tax return commensurate with the after-tax returns on other investments.

Securities with greater tax exposure should tend to produce greater pre-tax rates of return.

But is this true of stocks as well?

Stocks that pay big dividends expose their investors to the tax man. Dividends are taxed as received.

Stocks that don't pay dividends produce their returns in the form of capital gains. The tax on capital gains can be postponed, because it isn't assessed until the gain is realized. In addition, under the old tax law, a long-term gain was taxed at a lower rate. So a gain had a double advantage relative to a dividend.

As a stock pays out more and more of its income as dividends, the fraction of the expected return that comes as dividends increases relative to the fraction that comes as capital gains.

If after-tax returns on different stocks are to be commensurate with respect to each other, the pre-tax expected rates of return on high-dividend-paying stocks should be greater than on low-dividend-paying stocks.

This is the theory of the *tax premium*.

There is another, however. Merton Miller and Myron Scholes of the University of Chicago and Stanford University, respectively, don't believe in tax premiums (1978). In essence, they believe that it's relatively easy and costless to obtain tax deductions to shelter dividend income.

So you've bought a stock and have some dividends as a result. Don't want to pay taxes on them? Simple. Borrow some money and invest it in some other tax-sheltered investment. Maybe insurance. You can use the interest on the borrowed funds as a deduction to offset the dividend income.

Of course, this theory seems to break down when you ask the questions: "If it's this easy to avoid paying taxes on dividends, why do people pay taxes on any investment income at all? Why do corporate bonds sell at higher yields than municipal bonds?"

It's probably safe to say that tax deductions are not costless. And while it's certainly possible to avoid the tax bite on dividends, doing so may cause you considerable discomfort.

In any case, we've got two theories. One says that sheltering dividend income isn't easy. As a consequence, stocks with big dividend payouts will sell at lower prices consistent with higher pre-tax *expected future* rates of return. This is to compensate for the bigger tax bite. The other theory says that sheltering dividends *is* easy. And, because it is, stocks of equal risk will sell at the same expected rates of return, regardless of how much income is paid out as dividends.

Now there was a great debate between the two schools of thought. The leaders of the two camps were Robert Litzenberger, and Krishna Ramaswamy, from Wharton, who think tax premiums exist; and Merton Miller and Myron Scholes from Stanford, who think they don't exist.

LR versus MS.

Both camps spun their computers like mad. They were trying to find out whether, in a given month, the stocks that paid more dividends tended to produce higher rates of return.

LR fired first.

Their evidence (1979) indicated that you could predict before-tax stock returns on the basis of dividend yield (the ratio of the stock's quarterly dividend to its market price). Going into a month, you could expect that the stocks with the bigger dividend yields were going to have (on average) the bigger rates of return. This is to compensate their investors for the bigger tax bite.

MS counterpunched.

They (1982) argued that LR's results stemmed mostly from the stocks that paid no dividends at all. Many of these were expected to pay a dividend in the month but skipped it, probably because the company wasn't faring too well. The skipped dividend was an unexpected piece of bad news. As a result, the stock prices went down, producing low returns in the month. It was this, they said, that produced the overall result that low- or no-dividend-paying stocks tended to have lower than average rates of return.

LR reeled under the attack, but then struck back.

They refined their estimate of the expected dividend. Rather than use the *actual* dividend paid during the month, they used a model to predict what the dividend was going to be. They then used the predicted dividend in computing the new dividend yield. A stock with an unexpected skipped dividend would still be assigned its expected dividend yield in the revised study. The results of the revised study (1982) turned out to be pretty much the same.

All this debate was going on in the midst of the January upheaval. Predictably, someone was going to ask, "Is the dividend premium any different in January, like everything else seems to be?"

The person that asked this question was our friend Donald Keim.

Keim (1985) looked at monthly returns on most of the New York

Stock Exchange stocks in the period 1931 through 1978. For each stock he computed the dividend yield on the basis of total dividends paid during the year *preceding* the month returns are measured. Note that this is different from LR. They looked at the dividend paid, or expected to be paid, *in* the month the returns were measured.

In any case, Keim divided his stocks into six groups. The first group included all the stocks that paid no dividends at all during the previous year. The next five groups were all dividend-paying stocks, ranging from stocks with the smallest dividends (lowest) through the intermediate groups, to the stocks with the largest dividends (highest).

Then he separated his months on the basis of the calendar, January versus the other months of the year. In January could you predict that the returns to the stocks in the different groups would average dividends bigger, the bigger the average average dividend yield for the group.

And does January look like the rest of the year?

Keim's startling answers to these questions are in Figure 3–15. Unbelievable!

Absolutely nothing seems to be going on during the rest of the year. See, MS were right after all.

But look at January. This is a grotesque distortion of the world of LR.

For stocks that pay dividend returns do get bigger with the size of the dividend yield. This is the *tax premium*. Get more dividends. Pay more taxes. Want a higher return before taxes.

But look at the stocks that pay *no* dividends.

The *monthly* returns on these stocks average a WHOPPING 10 percent!

That's 10 percent in *one* month.[9]

Why should stocks that pay no dividends at all command such high rates of return? Is it because investors *really* don't like to get *no* dividends at all? And why don't they command returns like these in the other months of the year? Why don't they mind then?

There's something else that's peculiar about these results.

The relationship between the extra return earned and the dividend yield is too strong to be explained by taxes. Suppose we have two stocks that are identical in every respect save dividend yield. According to Keim's results for the period 1957 through 1978, if one stock has a 5 percent dividend yield and the other has a 6 percent

FIGURE 3–15 Tax Premium in Stock Market

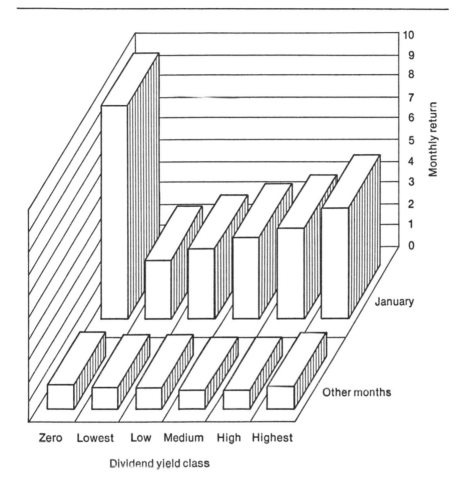

yield, we should expect the 6-percent stock to produce an additional 1.2 percent in January.

A 1 percent increase in dividend yield brings a 1.2 percent increase in pre-tax expected return.

This means you're indifferent between investing in the two stocks if you are in the 120 percent income tax bracket.

But there is no such bracket.

It looks like the premium we're seeing in the return may be induced by something other than taxes.

But whatever is inducing the premium, why does it come only in January?

Like the risk premium.

Like the correction of overreaction.

Why is *all* the action in January?

Why is January so *special*?

Why?

ENDNOTES

1. There are today quite a number of market indexes that give substantial weight to small companies such as the OTC Composite, AMEX, and Value Line. However, these indexes are, in general, more recent and receive less attention.

2. Beaver and Morse (1978) discuss the persistence of earnings growth and the relationship between earnings growth and P/E.

3. In a recent *Journal of Finance* paper, Banz and Breen (1986) claim that the data used by most researchers in the area of the P/E effect suffered from a number of biases. The first bias is the ex-post selection bias, and it arises because the Compustat data base contains only companies which are currently viable entities and have some history. The second bias is the look-ahead bias. At the end of the year we have a price, but the earnings for this year are available to investors sometime later in the next year. In many of the studies, the P/E (or E/P) ratios were computed under the assumption that at the end of the year investors know the reported earnings. Banz and Breen correct for these possible biases and conclude, "Thus, the ex-postselection bias and the look-ahead bias appear to create the 'low P/E' effect." However, looking at their results and given the bulk of the previous evidence, such a conclusion seems to be premature. Even in their results, low-P/E companies tend to outperform high-P/E companies. For each of five size groups, they compare returns on low-P/E stocks to returns on high-P/E stocks, and the differences in returns for none of the groups are significant at the 5 percent level. However, if they would aggregate their results across the five size groups, the results would tend to be significant. We actually feel that their results are supportive of the P/E effect. The most important size group is group 1, which includes the 20 percent largest companies or practically all the market value of equity. Based on their Table VI, low-P/E companies outperform high-P/E companies by .66 percent to .83 percent per month after performing adjustments for the biases. The range of T-statistics is 1.48 to 1.84. A rate of return of .66 percent per month is equivalent to an annual rate of return of around 8 percent per year. It is quite a difference in performance between low- and high-P/E stocks. Banz and Breen examined a much shorter period of time than in many previous studies—eight years. Because of the high volatility of stocks, even an 8 percent difference over a period of eight years is not enough to achieve statistical significance. However, it seems very likely that if they would examine a longer period of

time, as in many of the previous studies, the results would become statistically significant.

4. A more recent study by Cook and Rozeff (1984) provides strong support for the existence of both the P/E and the size effects.

5. More recent studies by Blume and Stambaugh (1983) and Roll (1983) reveal that when a feasible trading strategy is implemented (Buy and hold strategy), practically all of the size effect is concentrated in the month of January.

6. Rosenberg and Rudd (1982), and Rosenberg, Reid, and Lanstein (1985) develop a trading strategy in which they invest in companies that did poorly in the previous month and take short position in companies that did well in the previous month. Their results reveal substantial abnormal returns more than 1 percent per month. It is interesting to note that the highest abnormal returns are achieved in January.

7. Chan (1987) and Vermaelen and Verstinge (1986) pointed out some biases in computing betas during periods of extreme performance or, betas vary with changes in market values. To avoid this bias they estimated betas for winners and losers during the test period. Their results reveal that computing betas during the test period eliminates a substantial part of the extra returns. However, De Bondt and Thaler (1987) found that their arbitrage portfolio (losers-winners) has positive betas when the market goes up and negative betas when the market goes down. The interpretation of the results is that the arbitrage portfolio does well when the market goes up and well when the market goes down. Hence, it seems to be a very attractive portfolio and standard risk-adjustment procedures are meaningless for such a unique portfolio.

8. We should keep in mind that rates of return on common stock are very volatile, and therefore it is very difficult to distinguish between the various hypotheses; Even a 20-year period then is actually quite short.

9. *Some* of this difference is attributable to the fact that nondividend-paying stocks are usually small companies.

_____

CHAPTER FOUR

The Name of the GAME

WHY.

Buzzzzzzz.

Slow down—*just* a bit. An easy roll to the right. A sharp bank to the left and

      d

        o

          w

          n

       t

      o

     l

    a

     n

        d on the size 12 shoe propped on the desk of Sam Witherspoon, district attorney for Peach County.

Who didn't care about the fly on his shoe.

Because he was engrossed in a book about January.

" . . . why does the tax premium come only in January?
Like the risk premium.
Like the correction of the overreaction.

Why is *all* the action in January?
Why is January so special?
Why?"

"Easy. They're manipulating stock prices. That's why!"
Sam looked up at his shoe, wiggled off the fly, and turned to his assistant D.A., Fred Fowler.
"They're manipulating stock prices, Fred!"
"Who's manipulating stock prices?"
"The IRS, that's who. They've been doing it all this time right under our noses. Sucking the last drop of blood from our bodies!"
"Come off it, Sam. You and the IRS. That's all you think about. Get off their case. You can't touch 'em. They're beyond the law. At least, *your* law. You ought'a know that by now. Forget it!"
What was left of Sam's blood began to boil again.
"Forget it? Look. Seven audits in a row. SEVEN audits! My money, my houses, ALL my land. GONE! And *you* tell *me* to forget it? You'd better start re-thinking this situation, 'cause I'm not going to forget it. Ever!"
"Look. Ya still got your Cadillac, don't ya? Besides, you've done pretty well here in Peach County over the years, with all the 'deals' you've had goin' on the side."
'Never you mind about my 'deals', and don't worry—my Caddy's going *this* year in audit number eight! But let me tell you something. *This* year's going to be different. They may get a piece of *my* hide, but I'm going to get a piece of *theirs* as well."
"How's that?"
"Manipulating stock prices is a felony in this state, Fred, and I think I can make a case against them that will *stick*."
"So why would the IRS manipulate stock prices?"
"To suck a few more drops of blood. That's why. Fred, what if they could figure out a way to make stocks produce all their premium returns in the course of a two-week period every year? Suppose you were holding some stock at the *end* of the two weeks. You *expect* to get nothing special on the stocks for the rest of the year. What are you going to do?"
"Sell 'em and put the money somewhere else, I s'pose. But what's your point?"
"Look. If you sell the stocks and realize the gains, they're going to *tax* you on them. More blood! And they're also going to tax you on

what you get from your other investment. Don't sell now and they'll only get you later when you do, and you'll lose out on the return on the other deal during the rest of the year. They're out to get you coming and going."

"But how're they gonna cram all the action in stocks into a two-week period?"

"The tricky devils have designed the tax law so that people sell stocks toward the end of the year. This selling pressure depresses market prices until the turn of the year, when it turns out they rebound, *in spades*!"

"But don't people save on taxes with their losses?"

"They've thought of that. There's a cap of $3,000 on net loss deductions, but there's no cap on taxable gains. True, they lose some revenue on the losses realized at the end of the year, but they pick up more on the gains realized at the beginning of the next. Net result, more blood!"

"But who's gonna buy the stocks I sell after the two weeks of action? Whoever buys em can't expect much in the way of return for the rest of the year."

"You can sell them to someone who hasn't read this here book I found, that's who! Fred, there are plenty of suckers out there waiting to be fleeced. The IRS just wants a *few* good men to draw a little more blood from. They don't have to draw more from everyone. Never fear; they'll get the others with some other scam."

"Sounds pretty farfetched to me, Sam. You'll never make it stick. Forget it. Give up. Remember—death and taxes."

"They may suck my blood until I die, but, before I die, I'm going to suck some of theirs. You just watch me!"

The 57-year-old chief prosecutor of Peach County picked up one of several 1040 forms on his desk and crumpled it into a ball.

He squeezed it.

Hard.

Harder.

No blood.

Yet!

OPENING REMARKS

"Hear ye. Hear ye. The Federal District Court of the United States of America is now in session; the Honorable Justice George P. Halloway presiding, the case of The People of Peach County v. the Director of the Internal Revenue Service of the United States of America."

BAM!!

Halloway's gavel stilled the courtroom.

"Ladies and gentlemen, we've spent the last two weeks assembling this fine panel of jurists. It's time we settle the issue before us. Let's proceed directly into your opening statements. The prosecuting attorney from Peach County will begin."

Sam Witherspoon *was* ready to begin. Ready to launch an attack based on seven months of research and travel to all parts of the country. The January book had given him a beginning. Leads. From there he had probed tenaciously through countless articles, followed by countless interviews. Finally he hit pay dirt—an Israeli professor named Josef Lakonishok, who recently joined the University of Illinois. Lakonishok knew probably as much about the January anomaly as anyone in the world. After talking with him for less than an hour, Witherspoon decided to build his entire case around him. A risky strategy. But one that could work.

He hadn't counted on being up against a woman, though. 'Specially one that look like *that*! Seems like the Feds aren't taking him seriously. She can't be more than 35 years old, for Pete's sake. Probably spent most of the last seven months in some health club.

He'd like to break her little neck.

One last look at his notes, and Sam rose to his feet and walked to the jury box.

"This is an unprecedented case. Take a look at them. The IRS is sitting in the *wrong* place. Usually, they're over there by *that* table where *my* folks are. Usually, one of *us*—you or me—is sitting by *this* table where *they* are. It's the *IRS* that's on trial *this* time. And *you* have the unique opportunity to see that justice is *finally* served."

Sam walked over to the three men representing the IRS "Take a good look at these guys. Look closely. When you look into their eyes, I want you to think of one thing. The 15th of April."

The voice of Tiffany Meyer rang like a bell. "Objection, your honor. This case involves price manipulation, not the validity of the income tax."

"Sustained. Take your case seriously, Mr. Witherspoon. You're an attorney, not a comedian."

"I wasn't joking, your honor."

Witherspoon turned back to face the 12 jurors. "But I'll get directly to my point. These folks are on trial for manipulating stock prices. I am going to bring a single witness to this stand who will prove, beyond a shadow of a doubt, that the following facts are true:

"First, that in January common stocks can be expected to produce a large fraction of their total return for the year. So large, in fact, that wise investors would be well advised to sell their stock holdings and invest in something else for the rest of the year. In doing so, of course, their gains become taxable, increasing revenue for the IRS.

"Second, that the stocks that go up in January are the stocks that performed poorly in the preceding year. These, of course, are candidates for year-end sales to realize losses for tax purposes.

"Third, that toward the end of December there is an unusual increase in *sales* of stock by individual investors. Again, tax-loss selling.

"Finally, that this unusual turn-of-the-year activity in the stock market began with the introduction of the income tax in 1917."

"In short, I am going to prove that the IRS provisions relating to the taxation of capital gains and losses lead to year-end instability in the stock market, and are designed to maximize revenue from the capital gains tax. These vampires are after every drop of blood they can get their thirsty tongues on!"

BAM!!!

"Watch it, Mr. Witherspoon."

"Sorry, your honor. I guess I got carried away, but I've said my piece."

As Sam retired to his table, he watched Tiffany Meyer stand to confront the jury.

"Ladies and gentlemen. Given the district attorney's checkered record with the Internal Revenue Service, I'm not surprised that Mr. Witherspoon is presenting his case with the *greatest* enthusiasm."

"OBJECTION!!!"

"Sustained. This is going to be your *last* warning on *that* one, Ms. Meyer."

"You can *count* on that, your honor.

"Let me present my case to you as simply as I can. My clients are innocent. The district attorney from Peach County is simply wrong.

I agree that something unusual is going on in the stock market at the turn of the year, but it's *not* caused by the provisions in the tax code. Indeed, I will prove that these same unusual events occur in countries that don't tax capital gains and losses and don't end their tax year in December. I will also show that these unusual events were occurring both before *and* after capital gains were taxed in many countries. Finally, I will bring in two key witnesses whose testimony will point in an entirely different direction to the *real* cause of the January anomaly."

With that, Tiffany Meyer turned from the jury, stopped, and locked eyes with Sam Witherspoon. Smiling confidently, she then returned to her table.

WITNESS FOR THE PROSECUTION

"Are you ready to begin your case, Mr. Witherspoon?"

"We are, your honor. I would like to call as my first and only witness, Professor Josef Lakonishok."

A mildly startled expression crossed the face of Josef Lakonishok. He hadn't expected to be called this quickly. Giving testimony wasn't a new experience for him, but he was a bit nervous. Nevertheless, he transferred his raincoat from his lap to his chair, picked up his set of exhibits, and began the long journey to the witness stand.

"Do you swear to tell the truth, the whole truth, and nothing but the truth, so help you God?"

"Yes."

"Professor Lakonishok, you are currently the Karnes professor at the University of Illinois. Is that correct?"

"Yes, it is."

"And is it true that you hold a Ph.D. in finance from Cornell University, and are considered one of the foremost experts on the subject of anomalous events in the securities markets, having thoroughly studied the work of your colleagues in the field, and having conducted, written, and published numerous studies of your own?"

"I do hold the degree from Cornell, and it is true that I consider myself an expert in this area."

"Will you then describe to this court, in your own words, the phenomenon known as the January Effect?"

"In this country, and in many others throughout the world, the common stocks of relatively small companies usually experience unusually large rates of return. This doesn't happen every year, mind you, but you can say that, in the first few weeks of the year, there is a significant increase in the expected rate of return to the common stocks of relatively small companies. In fact, so much so that a significant fraction of the total annual return is earned in those first few weeks."

"If you stayed in these stocks for the rest of the year, could you expect to earn a rate of return that exceeded what you could get, say, on a relatively low-risk investment?"

"Based on the evidence I've seen, I would say your expected return wouldn't be much greater than what you could earn on relatively low-risk securities."

"And what, in your opinion, is the principle cause of this "disturbance" in the stock market in the month of January?"

"Most experts think that the weight of the evidence seems to point to the conclusion that it is caused, at least in part, by investors who are attempting to realize capital losses in December for tax purposes. The selling pressure forces the prices of the stocks below their equilibrium values. The pressure continues throughout the latter part of December, and then is suddenly released in January when prices spring upward. It's like suddenly releasing downward pressure on a spring. The spring pops up."

"And why are small companies particularly susceptible to this pressure?"

"For the obvious reason. These stocks are thinly traded. When investors try to sell them to realize losses, there aren't a lot of other traders ready and willing to buy at current prices. So they must offer to sell at lower prices. As each additional tax-loss seller comes to the market trying to attract buyers, prices have to be discounted even more, finally resulting in a stock price that is considerably below its proper equilibrium value."

Sam could feel his witness gain confidence. Now he could get down to business.

"Is this idea of investors selling stocks at year-end to realize losses for tax purposes something new?"

"Hardly. It began shortly after the introduction of the income tax in 1917. Here, for example, is a clipping from the *Magazine of Wall Street* published December 25, 1920, describing the extent of selling attributable to the income tax."

"Your honor, I would like to offer this clipping into evidence as People's Exhibit 'A.' "

PEOPLE'S EXHIBIT "A"

Year-End Selling—A Feature

By G. C. Selden

. . . The 1920 holiday season has brought a greater variety of reasons for selling things, by a greater variety of people, than any previous year within the recollection of active business men. Some of these reasons are:

1. Some have had difficulty getting the spot cash to pay the fourth installment of the income tax. Some have had to jettison part of the cargo to do it.

* * * * *

5. A minor reason for selling of both goods and securities showing big losses from prices at which they were bought has been the effort to cut down on 1920 income taxes, to be paid next year.

Tiffany Meyer: "Objection, your honor. I would hardly call a newspaper clipping written nearly a half-century ago by some magazine feature writer reliable evidence in this case."

"Your honor, we are offering this evidence to show an awareness of year-end tax-loss selling shortly after the introduction of the income tax."

"I'll accept it as such, but I trust that the rest of your case is built on more solid ground, Mr. Witherspoon."

"My case is solid as a rock, your honor."

Sam turned to his witness and continued. "Based on this exhibit, we can see that people have been selling securities to realize losses for quite some time. But how do we know, professor, that sales of this type initially depress stock prices and subsequently result in the January Effect?"

"We can base this conclusion on a number of different studies. The very first was published in the *Journal of Business*, in 1942 by Sidney Wachtel. His evidence supported the hypothesis that the stocks that were the biggest losers for the previous year would do particularly well around the turn of the year. But there is an example of a more recent study published by Ben Branch in 1977. Branch looked at stocks which reach a yearly low during the week ending with the last Friday of the year. He then computed the average percentage increase in the price for these stocks for the first four weeks of the year. He found that they go up in price by 8 percent."

"And these stocks are likely candidates for tax-loss selling prior to the turn of the year. Is that correct, professor?"

"Yes, and to support the contention that losing stocks are, in fact, being sold in December, we have the results of a study by Edward Dyl, published in the same year in the *Journal of Finance*. Dyl looked at 100 stocks from 1960 through 1969. He showed that the stocks that *appreciated* by more than 20 percent in the first 11 months of the year showed a 12.5 percent *decrease* from their normal trading volume in December. The losing stocks that *depreciated* by more than 20 percent showed a 19.2 percent *increase* from their normal trading volume in December. I think we can conclude from this that investors are probably selling to realize tax losses."

Halloway interjected, "So you're saying that stocks that have come *down* in price are traded more actively at the end of the year."

"That's what the study shows, your honor."

Sam smiled. The judge was catching on. "And, professor, are all firms uniformly affected by this January disturbance?"

"Not at all. A study published by Marc Reinganum in the *Journal of Financial Economics* in 1983 shows clearly that it's the stocks of *little* companies that are primarily affected. In doing his study, Reinganum measured the tax-loss-selling potential for a stock by the ratio of its price at the end of December to the maximum price during the immediately preceding period over which gains could be treated as short term. This would be 6 months in some years and 12 in others, depending on the tax laws of the time. He regarded the stocks with the lowest year-end prices relative to their highs for the previous tax period as the most likely candidates for tax-loss selling. He then looked at the returns to these stocks (the 25 percent of the stocks with the lowest ratios) in January. Here, I've prepared a graph showing the results."

Sam placed the exhibit on a tripod next to the witness stand. "We would like to enter this as People's Exhibit 'B', your honor.

"Moving horizontally along the front of the graph, we go from the first to the seventh trading day in January. The set of columns in front represents the tax-loss-selling candidates that are also the 10 percent of firms of *largest* size. The set of columns in the back are the 10

People's Exhibit "B": The Reinganum Study (Losers)

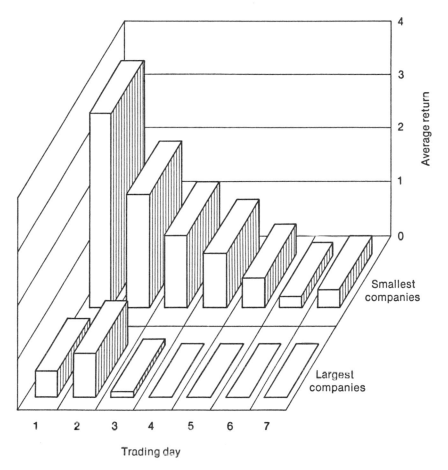

peicent coming from firms of *smallest* size. Note it's the little firms that really go up in January."

"And tell us, professor, do the stocks of little companies that did *well* in the previous period also go up in January?"

"Not by nearly as much. Here, take a look at this chart."

Sam replaced People's Exhibit "B" with "C" on the tripod.

"As you can see by *this* chart, which shows the same thing as Exhibit "B" but this time for the 25 percent of the stocks with the *highest* ratios of year-end stock price to previous high, they do go up a little, and the movement is more evenly distributed throughout January."

People's Exhibit "C": The Reinganum Study (Winners)

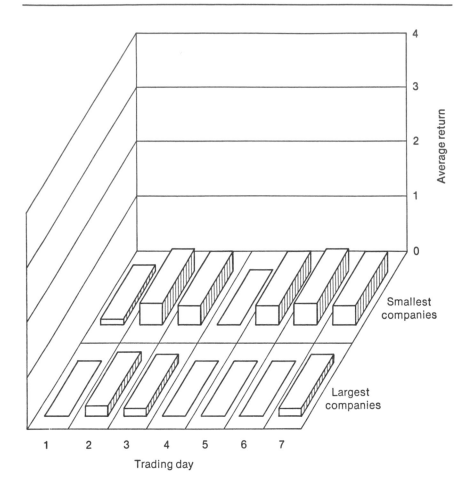

Another interjection by Halloway. "So the little companies are going up, but it's the little companies with poor performance in the previous year that are really on the move in the first four trading days."

"That's a fair statement of the facts, your honor."

"So let's see if I can summarize what you are telling us, professor. The stocks of little companies are the ones that go up in January. But *of* the stocks of little companies, it's the ones that performed most poorly in the preceding year that see the most action in January. Do you agree with this?"[1]

"Yes, I do."

Sam felt a slight tingle creep through his body.

Think of how it would feel to have a foot-long leech on your back for seven years. Slowly, very slowly, it sucks the blood from your body. Each year it becomes increasingly fat while you become increasingly lean. For seven years you can always feel it, but you can't get your hands on it. Now, suddenly, it's within your grasp. You can feel it with your fingers.

Question: Do you still have the strength to rip it off and kill it?

Or is it time to learn to live with it?

Sam Witherspoon would never learn to live with it!

But things were going well, he thought. Very well. Surprisingly well. And now he would introduce the evidence that would surely kill the leech.

"Well, professor, so far we've seen evidence supporting the notion that tax-loss-selling candidates perform well in January, but we haven't seen any evidence supporting *downward* pressure on their prices in December."

"I think I can help you with that. There is a recent study by Michael Rozeff, one of the fellows who first discovered the January Effect, by the way. He looks at returns on stocks in December, by size grouping. He divides the Decembers into years in which there is price *appreciation* between July and November on average for the size grouping and into years in which there is *depreciation*. Remember, in the depreciation years you would expect to see tax-loss-selling pressure in the group. Now take a look at this graph I've prepared."

Sam took the graph and carefully placed his prize on the tripod. "People's Exhibit 'D' ."

Lakonishok continued, "The striped bars show the December returns, by size group, that you would expect to see if prices went *down* in the same year from July through November. Note that for the smaller firms you expect prices to fall. The solid bars show what you'd expect if prices went *up* in the same year from July through November. In this case, you expect prices to go up for all size groups.

"This next graph shows the same thing, only this is for the following *January*. Note that you would expect prices to go up *more* if performance in the previous year was conducive to the tax-loss selling."

"We'll enter this one as People's Exhibit 'E'."

Halloway. "You've got those labeled as *expected* returns. Are those actual returns, or what?"

People's Exhibit "D": The Roseff Study (Dec.)

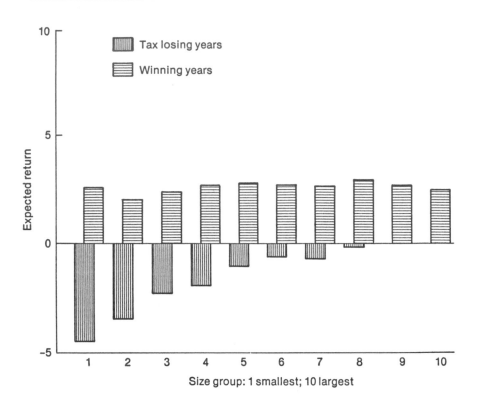

Size group: 1 smallest; 10 largest

"These numbers are based on a statistical analysis. The best way to interpret them is that they are the returns you would have expected to see for each group, *given* either appreciation or depreciation for July through November of the same year.

"If I might, I'd also like to add that in a separate study Rozeff found that non-members of the New York Stock Exchange shared a common pattern of having greater sales relative to purchases in December and greater purchases relative to sales in January. This result was consistent throughout the 23 years covered in his study. And no distinctive patterns showed up in any of the other months examined. What's more, in looking at patterns for odd-lot transactions, he found no distinctive differences between December and January in the period 1904 through 1940, a period when the income tax was non-existent or when tax rates were very low. But, when he

People's Exhibit "E": The Roseff Study (Jan.)

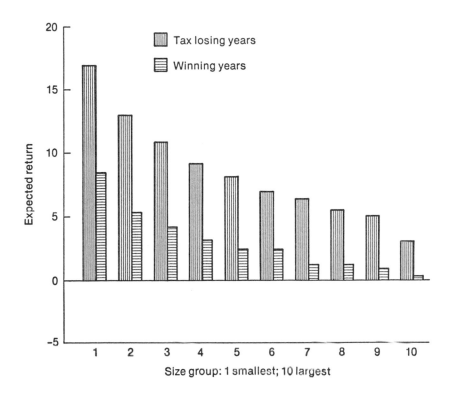

Size group: 1 smallest; 10 largest

looks at the period 1941 through 1982, the trading patterns for the two months become significantly different."

Halloway again. "So you're saying that, since the income tax has become a significant factor, non-members have been selling more in December and buying more in January."

Sam chirped, "I couldn't have put it better myself, your honor." He turned once again to his witness. "Is this the only study you know of that documents a distinct change in the year-end behavior of stock prices coinciding with the introduction of the income tax?"

"No. In a study published in 1985 in the *Journal of Finance*, Paul Schultz showed that the January Effect is really a post-IRS phenomenon. He looked at the difference between the return to a portfolio made up of stocks of small firms and the return to the Dow Jones

Industrial Average during periods running from the second-to-last trading day in December through the eighth trading day in January. The differences in the returns, by year, in the pre-IRS period, 1899 to 1917, is shown in this graph."

"Exhibit 'F'."

"On the other hand, the same differences for the period 1962 through 1980 are shown on *this* graph.

"We'll call this one People's Exhibit 'G'. I see what you mean. In the period *before* the income tax, small companies did better and sometimes they did worse than the Dow. January really wasn't a very special month at all back then, was it, professor?"

"It doesn't seem to be."

"But *since* the introduction of the income tax, January has been good to little companies in every year. Is that correct?"

People's Exhibit "F"

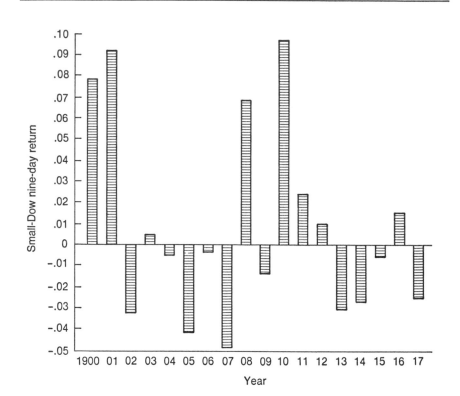

"At least in every year examined in this study."[2]

"Ladies and gentlemen of the jury, let me summarize what we've found. Little stocks that are candidates for tax-loss selling tend to go down in December and then up in January. This pattern has persisted since the introduction of the income tax, but the evidence indicates the absence of such a pattern before the introduction of the tax. Transactions data suggest that individual traders are selling in December and buying in January. The evidence suggests here, too, that they were doing this after income tax rates became significant, but not before."

Again, the bell, "Objection. Mr. Witherspoon will have ample time to summarize *his* case at the conclusion of *mine*.

"Sustained. Please save concluding remarks for their proper place."

People's Exhibit "G"

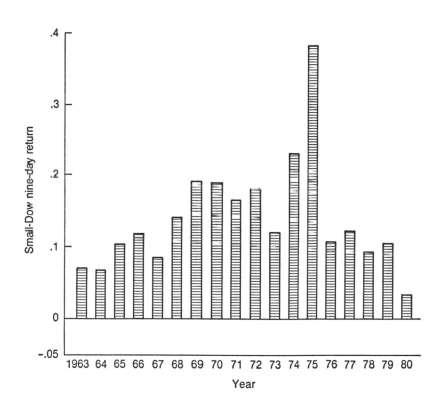

Sam felt he'd made his points. "I have no more questions of this witness, your honor."

Sam Witherspoon turned and faced his opponent. Not the opponent he would have picked, if he had the choice. He would have loved to have faced a beady-eyed, lean man, with long bony fingers, slicked-black hair, and a thin moustache. The kind of guy you faced in your last nightmare about your next tax audit.

To say the least, Tiffany Meyer didn't live up to that description. But he could live with that. In any case, now it's *her* turn.

Sam smiled confidently at Tiffany Meyer.

"The defence may cross-examine, *if* she wishes."

Tiffany confidently smiled back. Perhaps a litte *more* confidently, thought Sam.

"She wishes."

DOUBLE CROSS

Tiffany Meyer rose and crossed the 10 steps to the stand to confront Josef Lakonishok. "Professor Lakonishok, have you ever sold a stock in December to take advantage of a tax loss?"

"Yes, I think so. Several times."

"And when you sold, what did you do with the money?"

"Well, I usually invest it in something else."

"And *when* did you invest it in something else?"

"Well, right away. My broker has prepared lists of similar, alternate investments so that I can sell and then re-invest without changing the character of my portfolio."

"Did you ever sell in December to take a loss, and then *wait* until the following January to buy?"

"I may have."

"Is there any *reason* to wait until the following January to buy?"

"Well, it may take you some time to decide what you want to invest in."

"But there's no reason why you can't think about that *before* you sell, is there?"

"No."

"I mean, it's not a surprise that you are going to sell, and if you think about what you are going to buy *before* you sell you can save on lost interest, and then you only have to make *one* call on your broker. Isn't that right?"

"True enough, but for most people the lost interest and inconvenience may be a small matter."

"So you're saying that *most* people will sell and *then* sit around deciding what to buy. Then, all at the same time, in the first four days of January, they rush in to reinvest."

"The evidence seems to point to that conclusion."[3]

"Let's take another look at the evidence. Look with me at Exhibits 'D' and 'E'. Look at the vertical striped bars in 'D' and the vertical striped bars in 'E'. They show the expected returns for the stocks you claim are tax losers for the year. Right?"

"That's right."

"It seems to me that the January bars are roughly twice as large as the December bars for each size group. This means that these stocks go *up* by twice as much in January as they go *down* in December. If they're only recovering from December's price pressure, why should this be?"

"Some have argued that investors are taking their losses throughout the year as stock prices fall rather than wait until the end of the year."

"But these people wait until the beginning of the *next* year to buy?"

"That does seem somewhat unlikely, but another *possibility* is that, as these stocks fall from July through November, at least some of the December price pressure is anticipated in advance by the market and discounted into prices earlier; this argument is made in the literature."

"I see. You are saying that, if the market knows that price pressure is coming in December, it will discount the price in advance earlier in the year, at the same time as prices fall for these losing stocks."

"That's the argument."

"But this confuses me on two points. First, if this is true, why doesn't the market anticipate the January *increase*? Why does it anticipate only decreases and not increases? And second, I don't see how a decrease coming from *price pressure* can be discounted in advance. You're still going to have people coming into the market in December looking for buyers. If the stock is thinly traded, it will still have to be discounted to attract additional interested buyers. After all, it's not like anticipating the announcement of some news item in advance. You *can* anticipate that, and when the news comes in, it's not really news, at least to those traders who set the prices."

Sam Witherspoon cringed noticeably.

"That's a point, but what about short sellers? Anticipating the price pressure, they can short earlier and then buy stock from the tax-loss sellers as they cover their short sales later."

A smile from Sam.

"Professor Lakonishok, do you really believe short sellers time their transactions in this way?"

"I don't know. But they might."

"Professor, wouldn't you agree that this evidence points to the conclusion that there is some other force operating to produce the so-called January Effect?"

"I personally would agree that the January Effect is probably attributable to a number of different forces including, of course, year-end tax-loss selling."

More cringing, more noticeably.

"I am finished with this witness, your honor."

Sam Witherspoon had dust in his teeth. He had never been in a place like this before. In every direction there was nothing. *Nothing.* No mountains, no trees, no grass, no cars. Nothing. Just dust and sand. Right in the middle of the biggest desert he'd ever seen. Gee! Just him, these four Clydesdales, and *her.* It had been hard work calming those four big horses down. Took most of the morning to get them to stand here pointing north, east, west, and south. Easier tying the ropes going from her wrists and ankles to the harness of each horse. But now there she was, lying on her back, right in the middle of his own unique compass, ready to point, and then travel, to the four corners of the earth. Sam smiled as he slowly raised the pistol high into the air and fired . . .

"Any re-direct, Mr. Witherspoon?"

Gathering his composure, Sam appeared to speak with the greatest confidence. "One last question, your honor. Professor Lakonishok, are you still willing to state that the IRS code is at least in part responsible for the year-end disturbance in stock prices called the January Effect?"

"I believe the evidence points to that conclusion."

"That's all, I believe, we need to show. The prosecution rests its case, your honor!"

THE EMPIRE PLANS TO STRIKE BACK

It was 10:30 P.M. Tiffany Meyer and her partner, Jed Hirsch, made their way down the steps of the Federal District Court Building and walked at a fast pace to their hotel some five blocks away. The temperature was unusually warm, and the breeze was invigorating.

As they passed the streetlights lining the block, their shadows circled slowly from behind, stretched out before them, finally fading into the night, each replaced by another in succession.

"How are *you* feeling at this point, Jed?"

"I think we're in great shape, Tiff. I really think you took the air out of his sails. Lakonishok agreed right on the stand that this January disturbance is caused by factors other than tax-loss selling. For a while, I think I actually felt sorry for Sam in there today."

Even through her snarl, pearl-white teeth glistened in the lamplight.

"SORRY?!! You've *got* to be kidding! Sam Witherspoon is as corrupt as they come! You know as well as I that he's stolen millions from the people of this state over the last 20 years. Thank God the federal government was able to get some of it back from him. Congress should build a military base or something out here, so they can send the money back where it came from.

"Besides, I'm afraid it's not good enough to argue that there are other factors associated with this January thing. Maybe there are a lot of things going on at the end of the year; maybe tax-induced buying and selling is only one of them. But if he shows that the IRS contributes to year-end instability in stock prices, Witherspoon has made his case. He'll probably argue that the IRS knew about the other factors and decided to build on them to create the *level* of instability they needed."

"So what are you saying? We've got to show that the January Effect is *completely* unrelated to taxes?"

"Jed, I'm afraid that's exactly what I'm saying. And it's not going to be easy, either. Witherspoon's laid a pretty solid case supporting the notion that at least *some* of the instability is caused by the tax code. Besides, look at the jury we're facing. Do you think they regard us as counsel for the revenue-collecting agent of their government? If you do, you'd better think again. Those 12 people *want* to believe what Sam Witherspoon is saying. they *want* to believe that the only thing the IRS wants is every last penny they've got."

"Wow! You don't sound very optimistic about this."

"To tell you the truth, I'm not."

"Look, Tiff. I've seen you in a lot tighter spots than this. You've always scrambled out one way or another. You always find some kind of angle. So what's it going to be this time?"

"Well, first I'm going to try to show that this January thing is pervasive, even in countries that don't tax capital gains at year-end. That should strengthen my case that there's another cause for the disturbance."

"But how're you going to prove that the IRS isn't a contributing cause?"

"By showing that *all* of Witherspoon's evidence is consistent with another probable cause for the January Effect."

Tiffany Meyer reached into her purse and pulled a little book from one of the pockets.

"Take a look at this, Jed. I swiped this from Sam's desk as we left the courtroom this afternoon. It's a book about the January Effect, and I think Sam's been basing most of his case on it."

"*The Incredible January Effect.* What kind of a book is this, anyway? What's Witherspoon doing reading a novel in court?"

"I don't know what *I'd* call this book. But, in any case, there's a section in there about a study by two professors from Wisconsin and Cornell that interests me. Their results are really off the wall, but I think they can point the jury in a completely different direction. The more I think about this thing, the more convinced I become that something else is really behind the January Effect."

"Do you know what that something is?"

"Yes. It's not the IRS that's playing the game. The real players are the boys who push the money around on Wall Street, and I think I know how to prove it."

"How's that?"

"Bring one of them in and have him confess right on the stand, that's how."

As the two attorneys approached their hotel, Jed Hirsch continued to leaf through the pages of the January book.

"Tiff."

"What?"

"Have you looked at Chapter Four?"

THE DEFENSE FALTERS

Tiffany Meyer was pleased with the selection of her first witness. Seha Tinic, professor of finance at the University of Texas-Austin, presented the perfect image. Good looks, a commanding presence, distinguished, and old enough to look like he knew what he was talking about. In addition, Seha was from Turkey, and the trace of accent added to his presence on the stand.

"Professor Tinic, would you tell us in your owns words the results of your study of the turn of the year in the Canadian stock market?"

"Of course. My colleagues, Giovanni Barone-Adesi and Dick West, and I thought that Canada presented the perfect laboratory for determining the source of the January anomaly. You see, prior to 1972 capital gains weren't taxed in Canada. So if tax loss selling is, indeed, the principal cause, a January-type disturbance should begin after 1972."

"So you looked at monthly returns to Canadian stocks before and after 1972. Can you tell us what you found?"

"Well, Canada looks very much like the United States when it comes to January. Returns in general are unusually high, and this is especially true for smaller companies."

"And was this true in the period *before* 1972 as well as after?"

"Yes, it was."

"Tell us, professor, are there any *other* studies that confirm the results of *your* study?"

"Yes. There's a recently published study in the *Journal of Finance* by three professors named Berges, McConnell, and Schlarbaum—well, at least the first two are still professors. Schlarbaum has taken a professional position in the investments industry. In any case, they also show the presence of a January Effect in Canada both before and after 1972."

"Now professor, Mr. Witherspoon is going to ask you shortly about the *relative strengths* of the January Effect in the periods before and after 1972—"

"Objection! Counsel is putting words in my mouth. I am perfectly capable of asking my own questions, your honor."

"Sustained. Stick to *your* questions, Ms. Meyer."

"Very well, your honor. In the Berges-McConnell-Schlarbaum study, is there any difference in the relative January performance of small and large firms in the pre- and post-1972 periods?"

"No. In their study they were very much the same."

"And what about other countries that don't tax capital gains at all. Do we see a January Effect there?"

"Well, in Japan there is a January Effect very much like that in the United States, and capital gains aren't taxed at all in Japan. Also, in Australia the tax year ends on June 30. In spite of this, research shows abnormal returns of approximately 6 percent in January for small companies."

"So in *Canada*, where they began taxing capital gains in 1972, there existed a January Effect both before and after the tax change. In *Japan*, where they don't tax capital gains at all, there exists a January Effect very similar to that in the United States. And in *Australia*, where the tax year ends in June, there is still a disturbance in January. Is that a fair statement of the facts as you know them, professor?"

"I believe it is."

"Your witness, Mr. Witherspoon."

Sam nodded. He was glowing inside. This was going to be easy.

"Professor Tinic. Tell me, in your study did you find any evidence that the imposition of the capital gains tax had *any* effect on the seasonality of stock returns?"

"Well, yes. Unlike the other study I talked about, we did find evidence of a somewhat stronger January Effect after the change in the tax law in 1972."

"So *you* would conclude that the January Effect is, at least in part, tax-related."

"The evidence in *my* study is consistent with that, although I would argue that taxes are only *part* of the story."

"I am perfectly willing to accept that argument, professor."

"Let me state for the record now that I, Sam Witherspoon, believe that the IRS is only in *part* responsible for the disturbance in January."

Sam slowly made his way to the table for the defense and smiled as he looked directly into the eyes of Tiffany Meyer.

With his back to the witness, "And professor, about Australia, you say that the tax year ends there in June. Tell me, do they find an abnormal return in July in the Australian stock market?"

Still locked on those lovely green eyes, Sam didn't move a muscle as he patiently waited for the reply. Tiffany Meyer would always remember the smile he had on his face. It reminded her of the way Jack Palance smiled—just as he blew away the out-gunned home-steader on the muddy street of the movie *Shane*. For the first time she thought she could see deep into the black soul of Sam Witherspoon.

"As a matter of fact, they do. They find an abnormal return of about 3 percent in July."

"So this evidence supports the notion that the capital gains tax may be disturbing stock prices in Australia, as well."

"It would probably be difficult to find another explanation for the July abnormal return."

Sam didn't have his hands around her little neck, but he could feel them there anyway. He squeezed extra tightly before he turned to face the witness.

"And now let's talk about Japan. You say that there is no tax on capital gains in Japan. But tell me, are the *only* people who trade in the Japanese stock market the *citizens* of Japan?"

"No. Of course not. Foreigners trade there as well."

"And most of these foreigners pay taxes on capital gains in their home countries. Isn't that right?"

"Some of them do."

"So foreigners may be selling in December to realize losses to cover themselves at home—right?"

"This might be true, but I'm not sure how important that might be."

"But you can't dismiss the possibility that prices may be affected by this, can you?"

"I can't completely dismiss it, no."

"I have no more questions. Counsel for the defense may cross-examine my wit—excuse me—her witness, if she wishes."

Laughter.

Things had not gone well.

"Professor Tinic, as we discussed this morning, I knew that Mr. Witherspoon was going to raise the issue of foreign trading in Japan. So we prepared the following exhibit, didn't we? I would like to enter this as Defense Exhibit 'A', your honor."

As Tiffany Meyer placed the exhibit on the tripod, Sam angrily turned to his assistant D.A. "Fred, how in blazes did she know I was going to ask that?"

Defense Exhibit "A" (correlation between returns to Japanese and U.S. stocks—by study)

Study	Period	Correlation Coefficient
Grubel	1/59–12/66	.11
Solnik	3/66–4/71	.19
Lessard	1/59–10/73	.13
Koenenman-Bergstrom	1/69–12/78	.32
Solnik	1/71–12/80	.11
Ibbotson-Cass-Robinson	1/60–12/80	.22

"Got me Sam. I didn't tell her. Honest!"

Tiffany Meyer continued. "These are all the results of studies done by different professors whose names are provided in the first column. Isn't that right?"

"Yes. The time periods covered by the studies are given in the second column. The final column shows the correlation between the returns to stocks in Japan with those in the United States."

"Tell us about these correlation coefficients, professor."

"Well, the maximum *possible* value for the coefficient is 1. We call this perfect correlation. In this case U.S. and Japanese stock returns would move in perfect tandem. On the other hand, if the correlation were 0, there would be no association at all between the returns in the two markets."

"And what would you say about the actual degree of association we see here between the returns."

"It's quite low. Quite low indeed."

"Then this evidence is consistent with the notion that Japanese stock prices are affected by events that are peculiar, at least for the most part, to Japan. Is that right?"

"Yes. If Japanese and U.S. stocks were being affected by common forces, I would expect the correlation coefficients to be much higher."

"What, in your opinion, is the probability that stocks in Japan are affected by the U.S. income tax, or for that matter by the income tax in any other country?"

"In my opinion, that probability would be very low."

"And in your study of the Canadian stock market, did you investigate the possibility of seasonal, tax-induced trading activity by U.S. investors?"

"As a mater of fact, I did. I found no evidence supporting the notion that there is unusual trading activity in Canada at year-end by U.S. investors."

"I'm finished with this witness, your honor."

THE KEY TO THE LOCK

"Tiff, I'd like you to meet Werner De Bondt."

"How do you *do*, Werner? I've been very interested in your work. It's a pleasure to finally meet you in person."

He was a bit on the young side. Younger-looking than she had expected. Maybe too young. She wondered how he would hold up under Witherspoon's inevitable counterattack.

"Well, it's a pleasure to meet you, Tiffany. I hope I'll be able to be of some help to you."

Being from Belgium, he had a foreign accent. How will that come across? Probably will help to counter the age factor.

"Werner, we need some help right now. Sam Witherspoon's cross-examination's a bit tougher than I expected."

She looked at De Bondt hard, right through the eyes. Time for some motivation. Time for the "Gipper" speech.

"Werner, your testimony is *vital* to my case. It may not be abundantly clear to everyone yet, but what we've got here is a great jigsaw puzzle with all the pieces locked into place but two. You are the next to lock in. The final piece is due in here this afternoon."

Jed Hirsch beamed at his partner. She's got it. She's found the angle.

Werner De Bondt smiled confidently. "Don't worry, Tiffany. I love puzzles. Just lead me to my slot, and watch me lock into place."

"Right through that door, Werner. Right through that door."

"After you, Ms. Meyer."

BAM!!!

"Are you ready to proceed this morning, Ms. Meyer?"

"I am, your honor. I would like to call Werner De Bondt as my next witness."

Werner was sworn in, and Tiffany Meyer proceeded through the preliminaries, establishing De Bondt's credentials as an assistant professor of finance at the University of Wisconsin, with a Ph.D. from Cornell University. Now to place the key in the lock.

"Professor De Bondt, you have been working for several years on studies relating the behavior of stock prices, especially the subsequent behavior of stocks that have exhibited unusually good or poor performance in past periods. Is that correct?"

"Yes. It's my contention that the stock market overreacts to events. Stock prices are pushed too high on receipt of good information, and too low on the receipt of bad. If this is true, the stocks with the best performance in past periods should be expected to perform poorly in the future as their prices come down to equilibrium levels. Conversely, the worst stocks of the past should be expected to do well in the future."

"And does your research show that this is indeed the case?"

"It does, but with a surprising twist. The movement toward equilibrium seems to come in one month. The month of January. Past losers take a sharp jump up in the next January, and past winners take a jump down."

"But, contrary to losers, winners don't take a *sharp* jump down. Correct?"

"That's right. It's not symmetric. There's a much bigger jump *up* for the undervalued stocks in January than a jump *down* for the overvalued stocks. This has always puzzled me."

"And, professor, isn't it the case that your research also shows that the stocks that have previously done very well in the market (the winners) also show a tendency to rise in value in *subsequent* year-end periods?"

"That's absolutely correct. Previous winners have a tendency to rise in value in October, November, and December."

"Very interesting, Professor De Bondt. Tell me—these winners, their market prices are likely to be quite high relative to current earnings and dividends per share, isn't that right?"

"Yes, I would expect that to be the case."

"And the losers—these are the stocks that the market is most pessimistic about. You would expect their prices to be depressed relative to current earnings and dividends?"

"True. Actually, there is another study by a professor named Basu which is quite consistent with our results."

Tiffany hesitated. She recalled something about Basu from the

January book. But her recollection was fuzzy. Should she pursue?
Let's go. "Really, professor? Tell us about it."

"Basu examined the performance of stocks with high and low
price-earnings ratios and found that stocks with low price-earnings
ratios outperformed their counterparts with high P/Es."

Bingo!

"Professor, wouldn't stocks with low price-earnings ratios also
have low price-dividend ratios or high dividend yields?"

"Yes, I believe they probably would."

Another draw from the January book. "Professor, do you know
of any study which shows that stocks with high dividend yields perform unusually well in January?"

"As a matter of fact, there was a study by a fellow named Keim
which did show that high dividend yield stocks did unusually well in
January."

"But wasn't the relationship between dividend yield and performance too strong to be attributed entirely to taxes?"

"That's right. I believe his results were consistent with an ab-
surdly high marginal tax rate."

"Would you not agree, professor, that the results of Keim, Basu,
and yourself are consistent with the notion that the market is correct-
ing for a previous overreaction?"

"I hadn't thought of it that way, but that's an interesting
observation."

"And the correction comes in January?"

"Oddly enough, it seems to."

"And do you know of other research that shows that *risk premiums* are, for the most part, earned in January?"

"Yes. Several studies have shown that investors *do* earn higher
rates of return in risky stocks and bonds, but the puzzling thing is that
most of the extra return seems to come in January."

De Bondt smiled. "Believe me, we finance professors are really
having a tough time trying to come up with an explanation for that
one."

Tiffany Meyer had made the four points she needed to make, and
one extra for good measure. Risky securities do well in January.
Undervalued securities also do well in January. The asymmetry
between winners and losers. Upward pressure on the prices of previous winners toward the end of the year. And finally, researchers may

be confusing the so-called January tax premium with a correction of overreaction by the market.

A quick strike, and now, step back and hope.

"I'm finished, your honor."

The wind was blowing fiercely. Wow! Sam Witherspoon swayed at the top of El Capitan, an enormous rock towering over Yosemite Valley. Right on the edge! Better be *mighty* careful. Sam tied the wire to her ankle. The other end was tied to the tree next to him, with 50 feet of slack between the two ends. The wire was just the right gauge. Just *thick* enough so it wouldn't break at the end of her 50-foot fall. Just *thin* enough so it would slice immediately through her flesh, and then slowly through the bone, as she swayed back and forth in the wind. An agonizing wait for the inevitable completion of her trip down. He flashed his Jack Palance smile for her one last time. She deserved all that she was going to get. This was going to be one great afternoon!

. . . . .BAM!!! **BAM!!! BAM!!!**

"Mr. Witherspoon. Are you with us today.?"

"What? Oh. Of course I am, your honor. I was just putting my thoughts together."

Sam put *himself* together and walked over to Werner De Bondt.

"Professor De Bondt, do you have *any* explanation?"

"What do you mean, any explanation?"

"Any explanation as to why the stock market waits until January to correct its past mistakes. How do you explain this ritualistic behavior, anyway? Do you have *any* explanation?"

"Look, I admit that this behavior is difficult to explain, but I'm absolutely convinced that it's there."

"Oh, I'm absolutely convinced about that too, but unlike you, *I* have an explanation. *You* say the losing stocks of the past do well in January. *I* say they do well because tax loss selling forced their prices down prior to year-end. *You* say the winning stocks of the past do poorly in January. *I* say that's because people wait until January to sell them because they can delay paying capital gains taxes on their winnings until the end of the year. *Your* evidence fits very well with *my* story, doesn't it?"

Werner De Bondt: "But if the people holding winning stocks at the turn of the year wait until January to sell, why don't they wait even longer?"

"I'm talking about people who want out of the stocks in December. If they sell in December, they have to pay taxes on the gains right away. If they wait a little bit and sell in January, they don't have to pay their tax on the gain for a full year. Makes sense to *me*. I'm not talking about a mass movement here, but maybe that's why your results aren't symmetric. The winners don't come down in January as much as the losers go up."

"In any case, I've enjoyed your testimony, Professor De Bondt.

"I have no more questions of this witness, your honor."

As Sam Witherspoon marched confidently to his table, Tiffany Meyer turned to Jed Hirsch. "Don't worry, Jed. I knew he'd play that card. But we've still got the winning hand!"

"No re-direct, your honor."

THE FINAL PIECE

"I have a hostile witness, your honor."

"Very well, Ms. Meyer, you may ask him to take the stand."

"I would like to call, as my final witness, a Mr. Leif Grando "

"Will the Marshall-at-Arms please escort Mr. Grando to the stand?"

Grando thought, "What's going on here? Just because I'm a hostile witness doesn't mean I'm *hostile*!"

Obviously, Leif Grando didn't want to be there. He had received the subpoena the week before, and had tried every conceivable way to get out of it. Being involved with this ridiculous trial was *just* what he needed right now. As if things hadn't gone badly enough this year. But just wait till next year. He'd wow 'em again, just like he used to.

"Do you swear to tell the truth, the whole truth, and nothing *but* the truth, so help you God?"

"I do."

"Mr. Grando, are you, and have you, been employed as a portfolio manager for the past 10 years?"

"Yeah. I've been in the business that long."

"And, as a pension fund portfolio manager, you invest the pension fund's assets in a wide variety of investments, do you not?"

"That's my job."

"And these investments include stocks of both high and low risk, corporate bonds, again ranging in quality, and other investments. Correct?"

"That's right. I invest in lots of things."

"And you're *paid* to invest in these things."

"Of course I am."

"Just *how* are you paid?"

"Salary. Just like most everybody."

"And what are changes in the size of your salary based on?"

"My performance for the year."

"The return you earn on your portfolio?"

"As compared to the market, yeah. If I do better than the S&P 500, I usually get a nice raise for myself."

"And what if you do worse than the S&P 500?"

"Then I'm out of luck. No raise."

"What if you *really* do worse?"

"Well, if I *really* hit some bad notes, I could run into trouble."

"You mean like losing an account or maybe your job."

"Could happen."

"As you know, I took the liberty to have some of the records relating to your past performance subpoenaed last week. Do you recognize this as a printout of your portfolio holdings for calendar year 1981?"

"Yeah. That looks right."

"Let's take a look at the composition of your portfolio as of March 31, 1981. It looks like you're about 80 percent invested in stock, with the remaining 20 percent in corporate bonds. There are a few stocks in here I've heard of before, but there are many others I haven't."

"Well, if you're looking for bargains, like I usually am, the stocks of smaller, lesser-known companies are a good place to look—especially for the smaller pension funds, like the ones I manage. There's too much action in the big stocks. They get too much attention. Prices seldom get out of line. So when I'm looking for bargains, I go to smaller companies."

"And I see in your bond holdings a number of lower-quality issues, junk bonds."

"As a portfolio manager, I want to maximize my return, don't I?"

"If you want to maximize your salary, you do. Now let's look at this. This shows your portfolio holdings as of September 30, 1981. Your portfolio looks quite different here. Stocks are down to 65 percent of the total portfolio, and now I recognize most of these names. What happened to the smaller companies?"

"1981 was a great year for *me* anyway. Those small companies I was holding earlier in the year did really well. I earned my raise really early that year."

"So you sold them—the small companies."

"You bet."

"And what did you do with the proceeds of the sale?"

"I invested it in things like S&P 500 stocks and government bonds."

"To make sure you wouldn't lose the raise you had already earned. Right?"

"Look, I'm like everybody else. When you're a winner, you'd best walk away from the roulette table—at least, if you want to *stay* a winner. Besides, once you do as well as I did that year, doin' even better isn't gonna do much more for you. Know what I mean?"

"What you mean is that your compensation doesn't go up in direct proportion to your performance, right?"

"Yeah. If you're way out of line on the up side, people are likely to think you've been lucky, and you don't get paid for luck."

"So, Mr. Grando, if you've done well, the prospect of losing your realized performance means more to you than further gains."

"Yeah, I'd have to admit that."

"And so you realize your gains and lock them in."

"Listen, I know what I'm doin'."

"And what about *this* year? This hasn't been a very good year for you, has it?"

"Don't remind me."

"And what does the composition of your managed portfolios look like right now—in December?"

"I'm playing it pretty close to the vest right now. Like I said, I don't want to hit too many bad notes in one year. Besides, I've got to report the composition of my portfolios to my clients quarterly, but at the end-of-the-year report is especially important to them. Wouldn't want them to get excited by seeing some "marginal" investments in the portfolio they've never heard of before."

"You wouldn't want your clients to see a number of losing stocks in their portfolios at the end of the year, would you?"

"Tell me. Do I look stupid to you or somethin'? Losers hold losing stocks. I'm not a loser, lady. I get rid of them before I let them take the annual picture of my portfolio."

Tiffany Meyer turned and made her point facing Sam Witherspoon.

"So you would be culling the losers out at year end."

"That's what I said."

"Selling them in December."

Grando was becoming irritated. "How long are we gonna go around on this anyway? *Yes!*"

"And when you sell them, do you then invest the money by buying well-known stocks that have been doing particularly well in terms of their past performance?"

"Lady, who do *you* like to hang out with, losers or winners?"

"This pattern you have of playing it close to the vest toward the last few months of the year, is this typical for you?"

"Yeah, most of the time. 'Specially in years when I've played a lot of bad notes or really beautiful music."

"But in any given year there are probably many other managers like you who've played bad notes or beautiful music, even if *you* haven't. Right?"

"That's right, lady. It's a tough business. They rank us every year by our performance. You feel really good when you're on the top, but believe me, you're hurt'n when you're on the bottom."

"And when the year's over, what happens then?"

"What do you think happens? I've got to make a living, don't I? I go out after *next* year's raise. You *bet* I do. We *all* do."

"So you play your portfolios less close to the vest. You become more aggressive. You invest in risky stocks, risky bonds. But not just *any* risky stocks. Right?"

"Of course I don't just invest in *any* stocks. I invest in the stocks I think are going to do the *best* in the next year. The *undervalued* stocks."

"So in the first few days of the year you, and other managers like you, are out there hunting for bargains among the smaller stocks. You're trying to buy the stocks of smaller companies that you perceive to be *undervalued*."

Tiffany Meyer again turned to face Sam Witherspoon.

"Mr. Grando, this next question is *very* important. As you and your friends are buying these stocks, do you think you affect their prices?"

"Yeah. Lots of times my trades move the price. Especially for small companies."

"So, in the process of meeting the bids of you and your friends, these undervalued stocks may quickly become correctly valued?"

"You know the story. First one to dinner gets the white meat, last one gets the crumbs."

"That's a new one on me, Mr. Grando, but I know what you mean."

This was it. The cut was deep enough. Step back. The tree was ready to fall.

"Mr. Grando, let me tell you something. You, and people like you, are playing a GAME. Rather than looking out for the welfare of your *clients*, you're only looking out for *yourselves*. And your management reflects your motives. As you get what you want—or as there becomes a real danger of getting exactly what you *don't* want—you play the GAME close to the vest. But each of you begins playing that way at a different time of the year, depending on your individual experience *during* the year. Because you and your friends *exit* the risky, thinly traded side of the market at different times, the act of *exiting* doesn't make waves. But the GAME begins for all of you at precisely the same time—in the first few days of January. It's *then* that you move back. You move back to risky stocks. You move back to risky bonds. And, because you all move back at the *same time*, you affect *prices*.

"The prices of *risky* securities go up. *That's* why risk premiums are all earned in one month.

"And you're really after the *undervalued* stocks, so their prices go up the most. *That's* why it appears the market corrects its mistakes in one month. It's in January that you, and others like you, take your positions for the year. *That's* why the *undervalued* stocks go *up* so much in January, but the *overvalued* stocks hardly go *down* at all. You're not pushing on *them*, are you?

"And let me tell you something else. You and your friends on Wall Street aren't alone in this. You've got other friends on the other side of the earth. Performance is evaluated on a calendar-year basis nearly all over the world—even in countries where the tax year differs from the calendar year. This same GAME is being played everywhere, isn't it?"

"OBJECTION!"

"I strongly object, your honor. These are nothing but *wild* conjectures. There hasn't been a *shred* of evidence introduced in this case to support any of these allegations!"

Tiffany Meyer *knew* that was coming. *That's* what she had been waiting for. The look on her face silenced the entire courtroom. Suddenly, you could hear the clock ticking on the wall.

Those emerald green eyes locked with Sam Witherspoon's.

She walked triumphantly to his table.

Eyeball to eyeball, she tried her best to smile *just* like Jack Palance.

"Mr. Witherspoon, *that* is simply *not* true. You see, the weight of the evidence presented in this case, on your side as well as mine, supports *my* contention as well as *yours*. *You* say that the stocks of small companies with poor performance in the preceding year are the big winners in January. *I* say that fits *my* story precisely. *You* say that the January Effect can't be traced to the early part of the century. Well, *I* say the incentive system for portfolio managers wasn't widely employed then either. *You* say it's the income tax. *I* say it's a GAME. The plain truth of the matter is that we can't tell *which* of us is right on the basis of the evidence presented in this case."

Now she turned to the jury.

"And *you* must judge whether my clients are guilty *beyond a shadow of a doubt*. Can you find them guilty on those terms in the face of this alternate explanation? You *know* you can't. Not when the evidence that points to the income tax points just as clearly to my GAME."

And now she turned, and seemed to point to open space.

"And *you*, out there reading this book. Go back and take a look at the evidence presented in this trial. The income tax or the GAME? Which do you think is better supported?"

"Book? What book? Fred, who in blazes is she talking to? Is she crazy or something?"

"The defense rests."

EPILOGUE

Tiffany Meyer assembled her papers from the defense table for the last time and put them in her briefcase. Winning this case was a satisfying experience. A *really* satisfying experience. Especially considering her opponent.

Speaking of her opponent, how about a sweet goodbye?

She walked to the prosecution's table and offered her hand to Witherspoon.

"Sam, I just wanted to say that I thought you did a great job. You really surprised me."

A backhanded compliment wasn't exactly what he needed right now. "Listen, you haven't seen the last of this old boy yet. *Next time* will be different."

"Time will tell, Sam. Time will tell."

As Tiffany Meyer turned to leave, Sam stopped her. "Wait. Before you go, tell me one thing."

"What's that, Sam?"

"I got the feeling all through this trial that *you* knew what I was up to before *I* did."

"Did you, Sam?"

"That's right, I did. Now tell me, was it someone on my staff?"

"I didn't learn anything from your staff, Sam. But I'll give you some free advice."

Tiffany Meyer pulled the January book from her briefcase. "What's that?"

She tossed it the five feet to his table. It landed there, spun twice, and stopped right in front of Sam Witherspoon.

"Sam. *Next time*, finish the book!"

ENDNOTES

1. A paper by Givoly and Ovadia (1983) shows that even large companies that had extreme losses in the past had a remarkable performance in January.

2. Based on Ibbotson and Associates (1986) publication, which includes the period 1926 to 1985, an index of small stocks had a positive rate of return in January in 48 out of 60 years (80 percent of the time), and in 53 out of 60 years (88 percent), the small stock index outperformed the S&P 500. The average rate of return in January was 7.2 percent.

3. As indicated earlier, prices of small stocks start to go up on the last trading day of January.

Playing The GAME

WHAT WE KNOW

Before we decide what to do about all this, let's step back and review what we now know.

Something causes pressure on security prices at the beginning of the year. That "something" may be a combination of tax-loss selling and gamesmanship on the part of professional portfolio managers.

The price pressure isn't uniform across all securities. It seems to be more pronounced for:[1]

1. Small companies with common stock valued at something less than $200 million. Given the current level of the market relative to what it was when the small-firm effect was measured, we may want to update this figure to $300 million.
2. Common stocks that are currently selling at prices considerably below past levels.
3. Common stocks that do not pay dividends.
4. Lower-quality corporate bonds.

The January Effect isn't confined to the United States. It happens in most of the industrialized countries all over the world. This is important, because it's likely that investors in foreign countries are now less aware of the January Effect than investors in the United States, because the January Effect has received more publicity in this country.

If, and when, the Effect gets priced away here, you may still be able to take advantage of it by moving your investments abroad.[2]

The pressure begins on the last day of December, and it seems to dissipate by the middle of January.

As we said, the January Effect may be caused by money managers playing games with your money. Many of them may be playing the game not for you, but to line their own pockets.

You, however, can get your money back by beating *them* at their own game.

There are at least four ways for you to play the GAME.

First, you can play with *financial futures*. This is an easy way to play, and it doesn't require much capital. Beware. Because it's so easy to play this way, there are already many players. The prices of financial futures may already be affected. And, this game is very risky!

Second, you can play with *index options*. The rules of this game are a little more complicated, but there may not be as many other players to contend with.

Third, you can play with *mutual funds*. This is one of the easiest and least risky ways to play. It's less risky because positions in futures contracts are usually highly leveraged relative to your overall wealth position. After you get set up with mutual funds all you have to do is pick up the phone twice a year and switch from one segment of the mutual fund to another.

Finally, you can invest in *individual common stocks*. This will require the most effort on your part and the most capital. However, if you've got the time and the money, this is probably the way to squeeze the most out of the January Effect, because you can confine your investments to those that respond the most to the January price pressure.

Now let's learn the techniques of playing the GAME.

WHAT'S A FUTURES CONTRACT?

Playing with financial futures is easy, once you understand what a futures contract is.

Technically speaking, the *buyer* of a futures contract is obligated to buy the underlying commodity (pork bellies, Treasury bonds, or an index of stocks) at a stated price on, or before, the contract's expiration date. The price at which you must buy is called the *futures price*.

Remember, the futures price is *not* the value of the contract itself. It is the price at which you're contracting to buy or sell in the future.

If you *buy* a futures contract, you're obligated to buy the commodity addressed by the contract; if you *sell* the contract, you're obligated to sell the commodity. Most of the time, however, you never really go through with the actual purchase or sale. If you bought a futures contract, and you want out, you reverse the transaction by selling the contract. In fact, for the types of futures contracts used to play the January game (stock index futures), you never actually buy or sell the index with the contracts. Settlement is always in cash.

You may have entered into a contract like a futures contract already without knowing it.

Have you ever bought a house? Remember what you did when you made your offer to buy? You signed a contract that obligated you to buy the house at the closing date and at the offer price. The seller of the house signed the same contract. You were obligated to buy, and the seller was obligated to sell, at the price stated in the offer. You also probably put up some earnest money to help guarantee that you would meet the terms of the contract.

That offer is like a futures contract. The offer price is analogous to the futures price. There is, however, one important difference between the two contracts. In a futures contract, the futures price changes from day to day, and the buyer and seller are compensated accordingly.

To illustrate, suppose you signed an offer to buy a house for $100,000. A week later houses of the type you bought go up in price to $110,000. Your real estate agent comes to you and says, "In order to keep this contract current with the terms of other, contemporary contracts, we are going to increase the purchase price to $110,000. Okay?"

You're going to say, "Not okay!" Right?

But what if your Realtor says, "To compensate for the higher selling price the seller will give you $10,000 in cash."?

Now you might agree to the revision in terms.

This is what happens in a futures contract. Each day the price in the contract (the futures price) is changed to reflect the levels of the futures price in contemporary contracts, and the buyers and sellers of the contracts are compensated accordingly. If the futures price goes up, the buyer of the contract gets money, and the seller of the contract must come up with money. If future prices fall, the revision in the contract price favors the buyer, so, if this happens, the seller gets reimbursed and the buyer must pay for the privilege of having the futures price reduced.

So, if you take a position in a futures contract, you have cash added or subtracted from your account from day to day as the futures price rises and falls. They call this process *marking to market.*

How much does it cost you to take a position in a futures contract?

How much did it cost you *for the contract* that obligated you to buy the house? The *contract* cost you nothing. It does cost you to *execute* the contract at closing, but the contract itself is free. You do, however, have to put down some earnest money to convince the seller that you will meet the terms of the contract.

The same is true of a futures contract. It costs you nothing to take a position, but you do have to put up a margin to help guarantee execution.

To play the January game, you will be taking positions in stock index futures. Each contract controls 500 times the value of the stock index.[3] On the type of transaction required for playing the game, these contracts require a margin of $3,500 at the time the contract is purchased.

If you buy a contract with a future delivery price of $250, and the futures price goes to $260, the futures price for your contract will be changed from $250 to $260, and you will have $10 × 500 = $5,000 added to your account. If, instead, the futures price falls, you will have money subtracted from your account. If a sufficient amount is subtracted, they will ask you for more margin. This is a margin call.

The important thing to remember is, if you buy a futures contract, you're hoping the futures price goes up. If you sell a futures contract, you're hoping the futures price goes down.

PLAYING THE GAME WITH FUTURES

You can play by taking a spread position (buying one contract while selling another). Since there is really no futures contract that concentrates in small firms, the best way to play the game with futures is to buy the Value Line Index futures contracts and sell the Standard & Poor's 500 Index futures contracts.

Why a spread position? Because the January Effect doesn't predict a beginning-of-the-year rise in the stock market as a whole. It simply predicts that little companies will outperform large companies (although, in general, small companies do have positive returns in January). The market as a whole may well fall with disappointing economic news at the start of the year.

To protect yourself from this, you take a spread position.

You want to buy a futures contract (Value Line) that is greatly affected by small companies, and you want to sell a futures contract (the S&P) that is dominated by big companies.

The Value Line Index consists of about 1,700 individual stocks. The contribution of each stock to the value of the index is *approximately* equal. Because of the large number of stocks and the uniform contribution, the Value Line Index is relatively sensitive to the performance of small companies.[4]

The S&P Index consists of 500 large companies. Figure 5–1

FIGURE 5–1 The Top 50 Securities in Standard & Poor's 500-Stock Index (based on total market value outstanding, February 29, 1984)

Company	Percent of Total Value	Cumulative Percent of Total Value
International Business Machs.	5.86%	5.86%
Exxon Corp.	2.85	8.71
General Elec Co.	2.05	10.76
General Mtrs Corp.	1.86	12.62
Shell Oil Co.	1.50	14.11
American Tel & Teleq Co.	1.41	15.52
Standard Oil Co Ind.	1.32	16.84
Schlumberger Ltd.	1.24	18.08
Royal Dutch Pete Co.	1.16	19.24
Mobil Corp.	1.05	20.29
Sears Roebuck & Co.	1.04	21.33
Standard Oil Co. Calif.	1.01	22.34
Eastman Kodak Co.	0.98	23.32
Standard Oil Co. Ohio	0.97	24.29
Atlantic Richfield Co.	0.97	25.26
Du Pont E. I. De Nemours & Co.	0.96	26.23
Gulf Corp.	0.94	27.16
Texaco Inc.	0.87	28.03
Hewlett Packard Co.	0.80	28.84
Bellsouth Corp.	0.78	29.62

FIGURE 5-1 *(Concluded)*

Company	Percent of Total Value	Cumulative Percent of Total Value
Minnesota Mng & Mfg Co.	0.77	30.39
American Home Prods Corp.	0.71	31.10
Philip Morris Inc.	0.71	31.81
Procter & Gamble Co.	0.68	32.49
Coca Cola Co.	0.63	33.12
GTE Corp.	0.62	33.74
Ford Mtr Co. Del.	0.61	34.35
Merck & Co. Inc.	0.60	34.95
Bell Atlantic Corp.	0.59	35.54
Johnson & Johnson	0.57	36.11
Ameritech	0.56	36.67
Reynolds RJ Inds. Inc.	0.54	37.21
Bristol Meyers Co.	0.54	37.75
Pfizer Inc.	0.53	38.28
Dow Chem Co.	0.51	38.79
American Express Co.	0.51	39.31
Nynex Corp.	0.51	39.82
US West Inc.	0.50	40.32
Southwestern Bell Corp.	0.50	40.81
Phillips Pete Co.	0.50	41.31
Unocal Corp.	0.49	41.80
ITT Corp.	0.48	42.28
Tenneco Inc.	0.48	42.76
Pacific Telesis Group	0.47	43.23
Digital Equip Corp.	0.45	43.67
Abbott Labs	0.44	44.12
Texas Oil & Gas Corp.	0.44	44.56
Sun Inc.	0.44	45.00
Union Pac Corp.	0.44	45.43
Superior Oil Co.	0.42	45.85

SOURCE: Wells Fargo Investment Advisors.

shows the 50 largest stocks in the index and their relative contributions. In the S&P, these contributions are unequal and based on the relative size of each company. For example, IBM itself is roughly 6 percent of the index, and 46 percent of the index is made up of the largest 50 companies.

Value Line is more affected by small companies.

S&P is more affected by large companies.

We expect small companies to outperform large companies in January.

So we buy the Value Line futures and sell the S&P.

If both indexes go up, we win on Value Line and lose on S&P. But we expect to win more than we lose, and on balance we expect to come out ahead.

If both go down, we lose on Value Line and win on S&P. But the January price pressure should help support the prices of smaller stocks, and on balance we still should expect to come out ahead.

If you're operating on a small scale, you'll be buying and selling a single contract. However, if you're dealing big, you may want to take into account the fact the Value Line Index tends to be somewhat more volatile than the S&P.

Discussing the period 1980 through 1984, it has been estimated that if the S&P increased by 10 percent in 20 days, you would *expect* Value Line to rise by 11.2 percent. Given a decline of 1 percent in the S&P, we *expect* a 1.12 percent decline in Value Line. The move in Value Line can be *expected* to be 112 percent of the move in the S&P. We point out, however, that these statistics are based on all 12 months of the calendar year. It may be the case that the behavior in January is different.

To compensate for the different volatilities in the two indexes, you will want contracts controlling a greater position in the S&P than you could control with Value Line. For example, if you control $100,000 in Value Line, you will want to control $112,000 in the S&P. If you buy 100 in Value Line, you'll want 112 in the S&P.

This way, you've got a more perfect hedge against an adverse move in the market.

HAS THE FUTURES PLAY WORKED IN THE PAST?

Two researchers named Clark and Ziemba have back-tested this spread strategy over the 10 years 1976 and 1977 through 1985 and 1986.

Of course, the required futures contracts didn't exist over the entire period, so the results for the first seven years are based on the actual values for the indexes rather than actual futures prices. Their trading rule involves buying one Value Line contract and selling one S&P. The positions are opened on December 15 and closed on January 15 of each year[5] (to close a position, you simply reverse the transaction, selling the Value Line and buying the S&P).

Clark and Ziemba assumed a transactions cost for each position of $82.50. You can expect to pay as much as $200 at a full service broker and as little as $50 at a discount broker. The margin requirements are about $1,300 for the spreads they constructed.

The net profit on the trades for each year is given in Figure 5–2.

Not bad. And it's interesting to note that the gains don't seem to be melting away as the news about January spreads. However, we don't recommend waiting until the end of the year to set up your spread.[6] We now have one more year of results to report. The profit on the spread for 86/87 was $1,143.50.

A word of caution. We must stress the risk associated with this strategy. On 1986—1987, for example, holding the position for one additional day would have eliminated all profits. Also, as more people find out about this, the Value Line futures price may become overvalued relative to the S&P toward the turn of the year. To see if it is, you may want to perform the following check.

First, find the dividend yield for Value Line and S&P. This is the ratio of current dividends for the stocks in the index to the value of the index itself.[7]

Next, find the rate of interest on government bonds that mature around the maturity date for your futures contract. We recommend that you use the March contract, because futures with longer maturities are affected by additional factors.

For example, assume that the index value is 290. With a three-month contract, the three-month Treasury Bill rate is 5.6 percent (1.4

FIGURE 5–2	Net Profits on Future's Trades
Year	*Net Profit*
76/77	$1,387.50
77/78	$407.50
78/79	$477.50
79/80	$1,827.50
80/81	$947.50
81/82	$-22.50
82/83	$2,207.50
83/84	$547.50
84/85	$2,317.50
85/86	$1,617.50

percent quarterly), and the dividend yield is projected to be 3.2 percent (.8 percent quarterly) at the expiration of the contract.

Making the following computation, we get:

$$\text{INDEX VALUE} \times (1 + \text{INTEREST RATE} - \text{DIVIDEND YIELD})$$
$$290 \times (1.014 - .008) = 291.74$$

This should give you a rough idea of what the futures price on each index should be. You might want to make this computation on a series of days before you set up your trade. If you find that the Value Line futures price is climbing above this value (see footnote 4), and the S&P is falling below, be careful. The January Effect may be priced away in the futures market.

The S&P Futures Index is quite liquid, with around 80,000 contracts traded each day. Value Line is less liquid, with only 3,000 contracts per day.

There are also two other index futures with reasonable liquidity.

One is the Major Market Index, which closely tracks the Dow Jones Index, and the other is the NYSE composite. The NYSE is a value-weighted index of NYSE stocks.

Still another index with some potential is the SP OTC 250. This one is based on a portfolio of 250 over-the-counter stocks. But, at least at this point, there is very little trading in this contract.

PLAYING WITH INDEX OPTIONS

A typical option contract on an individual stock gives you the *right* to buy or sell 100 shares of stock at a specific price (called the striking price) before a specific date (called the expiration date).

There are two kinds of options. *Call* options give you the right to *buy* a stock at the striking price, and *put* options give you the right to *sell* at the striking price.

Options are truly just that. Whether you actually exercise them is up to you. You *should* exercise a call if, at the expiration date, the stock's market price is greater than the striking price. Suppose the striking price is $40 and the stock is selling for $50 when the option expires. The option gives you the right to acquire a share of stock for $40, and you can then turn around and immediately sell it for $50. If you own the call, you've got a contract that is worth $10.

Suppose, instead, it's a put option with the same striking price.

The put gives you the right to *sell* the stock for $40, but this right isn't worth anything, because you can always sell the stock in the market for $50. The put wouldn't be worth anything unless the market value of the stock fell below $40. For example, if the market value were $30, the put would be worth $10, because you could go out and buy a share of stock for $30 and then use your put to immediately sell it for $40.

Puts *increase* in value as the stocks behind them go *down* in price, and calls *increase* in value as the stocks go *up*.

You don't actually buy or sell an index with index options.

Rather, they are settled with cash. If you hold a call and the index is $10 over the striking price when the option expires, you receive $10 for each option you hold.

How do we play the January game with index options?

We'll again be trying to take advantage of the superior performance of small firms at the turn of the year. This time we'll pair the Value Line Index with the S&P 100, a value-weighted index of 100 large companies. In both cases we work with the options that expire in January. Longer maturities will only introduce unnecessary noise into the transaction.

The easiest route to take is to buy a call on the Value Line Index and a put on the S&P. That way, if both indexes go up, we will lose on the S&P put and win on the Value Line call, but, since we expect Value Line to outperform the S&P, we should come out with a net profit.

On the other hand, if both indexes should fall, we lose on the Value Line call and win on the S&P put. Again, since we expect S&P to fall more than Value Line, we should again come out with a net profit.

Before we go on, we need to talk briefly about in and out of the money options.

If the value of the index is above the striking price, a call option is said to be *in-the-money*. On the other hand, a put option is in the money if the index value is below the striking price. *Out-of-the-money* is merely the opposite of *in-the-money*.

When an option is well into the money, its value moves approximately dollar for dollar with the value of the index. Otherwise, the dollar changes in the option are considerably less than the dollar changes in the value of the index.

In setting up our spread positions in S&P and Value Line, we will want to work with *in-the-money* options. This is because we'll want both the put and the call to respond identically to changes in the value of the two underlying indexes.

As with the futures play, you may want to compensate for the fact that the Value Line Index is somewhat more volatile than the S&P. You can do this by buying more dollars of S&P puts than you buy Value Line calls. Based on the numbers given for the futures play, you should buy approximately 12 percent more S&P puts than you buy Value Line calls.

If you want to go through the trouble of setting up a special account with additional margin requirements, you can sell these options as well as buy them. Set up the account and you can access the sell side of the January options game. Here you sell a call option on the S&P and also sell a put option on Value Line. A rise in the market brings a loss on the S&P call (it went up, but you're on the sell side), and a gain on the Value Line put (it went down, but you're again on the sell side, so that's good news for you). With January price pressure, the gain should again exceed the loss.

With a market decline, the opposite should happen with the same pleasant net result.

Of course, you take positions on the buy and sell sides at the same time for the sake of reducing your risk.

Playing the game with options may have some advantages over playing with futures.

First, at least on the buy side of the game, our losses are limited to our investment, the cost of acquiring the put and the call. In the case of a futures strategy, you can lose much more than your initial margin investment.

Second, if you again restrict yourself to the buy side of the game, you will not be annoyed with margin calls.

Third, there may be fewer players to compete with in the options game.

On the other hand, the options game requires a greater investment and higher transactions costs. In addition, if one or more of your options begins to lose its in-the-money status, you will have to adjust your relative positions in the two options to stay hedged. This means you will lose more in commissions. In addition, the Value Line Index option has a trading volume of around 2,000 contracts a day. It includes puts and calls, three different expiration dates, and nine different striking prices. Hence, for a particular option, the market may not be very liquid, resulting in higher transactions costs.

Still, the options GAME is an alternative some of you may want to consider.

PLAYING WITH MUTUAL FUNDS

Due to the limited number of different contracts available, when we play the game with financial futures or index options, we can't concentrate on the smallest companies. Even the Value Line Index is affected to a large degree by the performance of the largest firms that are part of the index.

To provide for exclusive investments in smaller firms, we now shift our sights to mutual funds.

A mutual fund is actually a portfolio of investments. The total market value of the investments is calculated each day, and this total is divided by the number of shares outstanding in the fund. This is the price you must pay to acquire a share in the fund.

There are a number of mutual funds that specialize in investing in the stocks of smaller companies. Here's a partial list:

1. The Acorn Fund
2. Alger Small Capitalization Portfolio
3. Dreyfus New Leaders
4. Explorer II
5. Fidelity OTC
6. Price, Rowe New Horizons
7. Scudder Development Fund

Since smaller firms outperform larger firms only in January, the idea is to enter the fund at the end of December, and then move out again at the end of January. Most of the funds listed above have a telephone switch feature. If you sign up for this feature, You can pick up the telephone and ask to switch your investments from one of the fund's portfolio classifications to another. In most cases you pay no transactions costs in making such a switch. Since we know that stocks and bonds produce nearly all of their risk premiums in January, you may want to switch your funds to low-risk stocks and other low-risk investments for the rest of the year.

A word of caution. Unless these are tax-deferred investments, as you switch you will be realizing capital gains and losses for tax purposes. Consequently, you may want to confine this strategy to your tax-deferred retirement accounts. On these accounts, taxes on realized capital gains are also deferred. If you're operating with tax-deferred money, you may want to consider the fund's tax-exposed portfolios for the rest of the year. Otherwise a tax-exempt fund may be best for you if you're a higher-bracket investor.

Another word of caution. These funds may be playing the *other* side of the GAME. The composition of their portfolios are published at year-end. To the extent that they cull losers to dress up their appearance, they are getting out of the stocks that are likely to perform best in the next month. Check up on them. See if they have owned some losers in past Decembers. Look at their relative January performances.[8]

There is an interesting fund called Dimensional Fund Advisors Small Company Portfolio that we know doesn't play the other side of the GAME. Dimension is an index fund which invests in all publicly held small firms with total stock value of between $10 million and $100 million.[9] The fund doesn't trade much, and it spends a minimal amount on research. It's not trying to beat the small-firm market, but only trying to match it. The fund now has more than $1 billion in assets, and it has recently become available to individual investors through discount broker Charles Schwab. We should add that Dimensional has small capitalization funds for the U.K. and Japanese stocks as well.

Charles Schwab charges a one-way sales charge of $50 for a $10,000 transaction, $78 for $20,000, and $150 for anything above $56,000. In addition, there is an extra charge of 1 percent. This works out to about 1.78 percent for a $20,000 round trip transaction.

For further information on small-stock mutual funds, we recommend the following publications:

1. Weisenberger Investment Companies Service (Warren, Gorham and Lamont).
2. Handbook for No-Load Fund Investors (No-Load Fund Investors).
3. Lipper Mutual Fund Performance Analysis.

In looking through the first two sources, small firms can be found under the classification of maximum capital gains (Weisenberger) or aggressive growth (No-Load Fund Investors).

Lipper has a convenient separate category for mutual funds which specialize in small firms. It is also interesting to note that Barron's reports quarterly on performance for the various types of funds as classified by Lipper. Its report is usually published four to six weeks after the end of the quarter.

Don't forget that the January Effect is even more prevalent in foreign countries than it is in the United States. There are a number of no-load mutual funds that specialize in foreign stock investments. These include:

1. Fidelity Overseas
2. G.T. Pacific Growth Fund
3. Price, Rowe International
4. Scudder International
5. Vanguard World—International

While these funds concentrate in the bigger foreign companies, research shows that the January price pressure has an impact on larger firms as well in many foreign countries. While smaller firms do perform *better* in Japan and Australia, there is no difference between the big and small in January on the Amsterdam Stock Exchange.

Also remember that if you wish to avoid the gyrations that are inherent in common stock investments, you can hedge your exposure to equities in January by selling S&P index futures. Since each of these contracts controls 500 times the value of the index, your investment in the small-firm mutual fund would have to be about $150,000 to take advantage of this opportunity. Big-time investors will want to remember to adjust their positions in the futures contract to account for the relative volatilities of their mutual fund and the S&P.

We know that losing stocks are the best January performers. Unfortunately, there are presently no mutual funds that specialize in losing stocks.

This brings us to the final way to play the January GAME.

PLAYING WITH INDIVIDUAL STOCKS

When you invest in a mutual fund, you play by their rules. You own the stocks they want to buy, and they aren't always the best ones for the January GAME. With your own individual stocks, you can also play tax games more efficiently.

So you may want to build your own January portfolio.

Keep in mind, however, that if you go your own way, you're going to pay more in commissions. A typical financial institution fund will pay a round-trip (buy, then sell) commission of .7 percent of the investment on shares with a price between $15 and $20, and some may pay as little as .2 percent.

In contrast, your round-trip to buy 300 shares of a stock, at a price of $15 a share, will be about 5 percent if you use a full-service broker, and 2 percent if you use a discount broker. Increase the scale of the transaction to 500 shares at a price of $20 per share, and your round-trip commission falls to 1 percent.

Discount brokers will buy and sell stocks for you. No fancy advice. No fancy financial products. But they get the job done, and on a short-run investment like this one, it's probably the route to follow.

Shop around for the best price you can get. Here's a partial list of some discount brokers you may like to look into:

1. Brown and Company
2. Fidelity Brokerage Services
3. Charles Schwab & Company
4. Ovest
5. Vanguard Discount Brokerage Services

The brokerage commission is the service charge you pay to the person who actually executes the trade for you. That person, however, buys or sells the stock from a specialist or dealer, who makes a market in the stock and usually holds it in inventory or from another member of the exchange who is selling.

Specialists and dealers also make their money from a second source. This is an additional element of transactions costs—the bid-asked spread.

The bid price is the price the dealer is willing to pay you for shares you want to sell. The asked price is the price at which the dealer is willing to buy shares.

So, if you buy at the asked price and then immediately sell at the bid price you lose the difference.

The size of this market-maker's spread is larger for smaller companies. A recent paper by Thomas Loeb in the *Financial Analysts Journal* finds the following relationship (Figure 5–3) between the bid—asked spread and firm size.

The first lesson from this table is that you may want to avoid

FIGURE 5–3

Total Market Value of Stock (millions)	Percentage Spread
0–10	6.55%
10–25	4.07%
25–50	3.03%
50–75	1.86%
75–100	1.46%
100–500	1.13%
500–1,000	.76%
1,000–1,500	.65%
over 1,500	.52%

investing in the smallest companies. Sticking in the $100 million to $300 million range may make more sense.

There's another important word to keep in mind when you are buying and selling small companies.

The word is patience.

We talked earlier about a fund called Dimensional Fund Advisors Small Company Porfolio. This is the one that attempts to invest in firms with total stock valued between $10 million and $100 million. Dimensional instructs its brokers to buy stocks without initiating transactions. Sit and wait for a transaction to enter the market, and then take the other side of it. Don't be in a hurry to buy. Be patient.

As an individual investor, you aren't in a position to give your broker such instructions. But you can trade with something called "limit orders."

With a limit order, you set a price and instruct to trade only when the trade can be completed at a price that is at least as advantageous as that price.

With limit orders, you again must be patient. You may enter your orders two weeks prior to the close of the year on more stocks than you want to buy, and then close the remaining orders when you have reached a sufficient level of investment. This is a time-consuming procedure, but it may pay off for those with lots of funds to invest. Follow the same strategy on the sell side. After the 15th of January, when most of the action has already run its course, put your limit orders on the stocks you owned before.[10]

Patience also neutralizes the third element of transactions costs—price concession.

If you are in a rush to buy, and there is no one ready to sell, you will have to induce sellers to come into the market. How? By raising the price at which you are willing to buy, that's how. Same on the sell side. If you want to sell a lot of stock quickly, it's going to cost you. So take your time.

To summarize, you can economize on transactions costs if you:

1. Use a discount broker.
2. Have patience.
3. Restrict yourself to firms between $100 million and $300 million.

Now to pick the firms to buy.

First, you'll need some good sources of information. One readily available source is *The Wall Street Journal*. It provides the 52-week high and low with its price quotations. This will allow you to select losers—stocks with current prices far below their 52-week highs. You can also use the daily volume numbers as a guide to the size of the firm. A $100 million equity company will usually have a turnover less than 100 percent per year, which translates to $400,000 per trading day.

Standard & Poor's Stock Guide is a more complete source of information. Here you will find the total value of stock for each company, as well as the prices for each stock for the last couple of years.

Value Line Investment Survey provides a still more complete set of information covering about 1,700 companies. In addition, for those of you with access to a personal computer, Value Line has a relatively new product called "Value Screen Plus." With it you can automatically screen the 1,700 firms based on a number of different criteria.

IS THE JANUARY GAME STILL ALIVE?

How have small firms done in January in recent years?

Figure 5–4 shows the difference between the rates of return to an index of small firms and to the S&P 500 Index in January from 1926 to the present. The small-firm index is that of Ibbotson and Associates. Since 1982, this index is actually based on the returns achieved by Dimensional Fund Advisors Small Company Portfolio. This small-

FIGURE 5–4   Small Firm—S&P 500 Return (January, last 50 years)

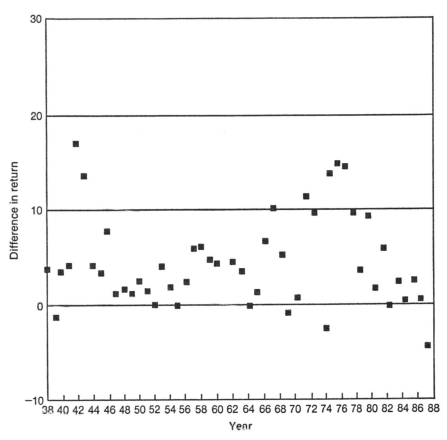

firm index is actually a total market value-weighted index of the smallest 20 percent of the firms on the NYSE plus stocks on the AMEX and the OTC with the same size range as the smallest 20 percent of NYSE stocks.

As you can see from the table, small firms produced larger returns than the S&P in seven out of the last eight years.[11]

What about the most recent Januaries?

Figure 5–5 shows returns for various stock indexes during the first two weeks in January. As you move down the list, the size of the average company in the index becomes smaller.

Note that small firms continue to outperform large firms at the turn of the year. Figure 5–6 shows that this was also true for the last trading day in December except for 1984.

FIGURE 5–5   Rates of Return for First Two
                 Weeks in January

	1985	1986	1987
DOW	1.59%	− 1.25%	9.22%
S&P	2.14	− 1.43	9.63
NYSE	2.29	− 1.20	9.75
NASDAC	4.22	+ 1.00	12.54

FIGURE 5–6   Rates of Return for
                 Last Trading Day in
                 December.

	1984	1985	1986
DOW	.61%	− .24%	− .66%
S&P	.59	+ .28	− .49
NYSE	.51	+ .32	− .39
NASDAC	.49	+ .56	− .43

January of 1987 was a unique example. The entire month witnessed an enormous bull market for stocks. The month had the largest gain in January in the history of the S&P index. The return is the second highest for any month for the last 47 years. But the nature of the market changed dramatically after the first two weeks. In the first half of the month, smaller companies led the way posting the biggest returns. But in the second half, the market turned around and the Blue Chips took over as the leaders. We have seen no conclusive evidence that the January Effect has been priced away in the United States. Furthermore, given the likely cause of the Effect, it may be around for some time.

A FINAL CAVEAT

It goes without saying that all of the strategies presented in this chapter are based on historical patterns of market behavior. These patterns may change over time. As an investor, you may be wise to keep in touch with the most recent publications relating to the January Effect, and adapt your investment strategies accordingly.

Investing to exploit the January Effect involves risk and, obviously, is not for everyone. It's important to keep in mind that the *expected* return to small companies seems to be higher in January. This is not to say that the *realized* return to small companies will be higher in every year. In some years, as in 1973, the reverse will be true. In years like these you will take losses playing the January GAME. You must be prepared to take these losses, for they are a part of the GAME as well.

We obviously make no guarantees that these strategies will work for *you*. We point out that, if employed intelligently, they would have worked in the past. Moreover, there is no conclusive evidence that they are less effective now than then.

As a final word, while we were putting this book to bed, we came across some interesting newspaper quotations.

The first is from *USA Today*. The date is December 29, 1986.

> . . . look for substantial buying of blue-chip stocks by pension and mutual funds. It's called window dressing: money managers buy stocks that have been strong recently, because of "fear of looking stupid" when clients review end-of-quarter portfolios, says Edward M. Kerschner, investment strategist at PaineWebber Group Inc.
>
> "You don't want to start 1987 with what looks like a dumb portfolio," he says.
>
> But while big investors concentrate on blue-chips, smaller stocks are likely to be forgotten until January. . . .

The second is from *The Wall Street Journal*. The date is January 12, 1987.

> Junk bond prices have staged a powerful rally recently, snapping out of a slump triggered by the Ivan Boesky insider-trading scandal.
>
> Prices of many junk bonds have surged back to or even above their levels of Nov. 14, when news of the Boesky case broke. In the past week alone, many issues have risen about three points, or $30 for each $1,000 face amount. That's far better than U.S. Treasury bonds did last week, although long-term Treasury bond prices have performed better since mid-November than most junk bonds.
>
> Many institutional investors are showing "strong interest" in junk bonds, said Martin S. Fridson, manager of credit research and a principal at Morgan Stanley & Co.

The third is also from the *Wall Street Journal*. The date is January 14, 1987. The title of the article is "Bargain Hunters Fuel Resurgence of Small Stocks."

What a difference two weeks has made. The OTC market in general has outpaced the New York Stock Exchange composite index and the Dow Jones Industrial Average since the beginning of January. Moreover, gains from the smallest issues traded through the National Association of Securities Dealers Automated Quotations System have done even better.

May the "force" be with you.

ENDNOTES

1. Not all of these effects are necessarily independent. For example, it is possible that controlling for size and past performance, we wouldn't find a dividend effect.

2. It's important to note that there are many anomalies which received much publicity and are still apparently not priced away. For example, the price-earnings ratio effect has been discussed for many years. In their seminal book, Graham and Dodd (1951) discuss P/E ratios as an indicator. Nicholson (1960, 1968) and Breen (1968) show that low-P/E stocks achieve high rates of return, and there are quite a number of additional, earlier studies in this area. However, based on recent results, the P/E effect still exists. Lakonishok and Smidt (1987) examine various seasonalities in the stock market by focusing on 90 years of daily data for the Dow Jones Index. It seems that the most publicized anomalies such as the weekend effect (negative rates of return on Mondays and higher rates of return on the last trading day of the week) and the holiday effect (high rates of return on the days before holidays) existed 90 years ago and shows up in the most recent data as well.

3. The Major Market Index (MMI) futures contract controls 250 times the value of the stock index.

4. The Value Line Index is actually based upon geometric means of relative price movements (the ratios of N ending to beginning prices are multiplied together and the Nth root of the product is found). Because the daily rate of return to the Value Line Index is based on a geometric average, this index has a downward drift relative to a computation based on a simple average. According to Clark and Ziemba (1986), the downward drift is about 5 percent per year, and it depends on the variability of the price movements of the component securities.

5. To execute these transactions, an investor can actually put a limit order on the spread. However, because the two contracts are traded at two different exchanges (Kansas City and Chicago), there is no guarantee that the transactions will be executed at prices at least as favorable as the limit. The day-to-day fluctuation in the spread can be substantial and, therefore, opening and closing your position with limit orders can have a substantial impact on the results. Clark and Ziembas' results are based on opening a spread through a limit order.

6. Of course, you should realize that the risk of your position is a function of the amount of time the position is open. A monthly standard deviation in return is about 4.6 times higher than a daily standard deviation.

7. The dividend yield for the Value Line Index can be found in the *Value Line Investment Survey* and the dividend yield on the S&P can be found in the *Standard and Poor's Current Statistics*. The dividend yield of the two groups are really not so different. The current annual dividend yield on the S&P is about 3.2 percent. Since there are no major quarterly seasonalities in dividend yield and our futures indexes have about one quarter until expiration, seasonalities in dividend yield can be ignored for all practical purposes.

8. Size is not the only criterion of most of the funds specializing in small stocks. In general, we do not have evidence which tells us how the additional criteria will affect their January performance.

9. This fund is a value-weighted index of the fifth quintile of the NYSE stocks plus the stocks on the AMEX and the OTC with the same total market value upper and lower bounds as the fifth quintile of NYSE stocks..

10. However, if new information is the dominant reason for trading, and there is a lot of insider trading going on, the danger of placing limit orders on more stocks than you intend to buy is that you may end up with stocks that subsequently decrease in price.

11. Adding the difference in returns for the last trading day of December would enhance the performance of small stocks.

BIBLIOGRAPHY

Amihud, Y., and H. Mendelson. "Asset Returns and the Bid-Asked Spread." *Journal of Financial Economics*, December 1986.

Arbel, A. "Generic Stocks, Information Deficiencies, and Market Anomalies." *Journal of Portfolio Management*, forthcoming.

Arbel, A., S. Carvell, and P. Strebel. "Giraffes, Institutions, and Neglected Firms." *Financial Analysts Journal*, May–June 1983.

Arbel, A., and P. Strebel. "Pay Attention to Neglected Firms." *The Journal of Portfolio Management*, Winter 1983.

Ariel, R. "A Monthly Effect in Stock Returns." *Journal of Financial Economics*, March 1987.

———. "High Stock Returns Before Holidays." Working paper, MIT, April 1985.

Bachrach, B., and D. Galai. "The Risk-Return Relationship and Stock Prices." *Journal of Financial and Quantitative Analysis*, June 1979.

Banz, R. "Evidence of Size-Effect on the London Stock Exchange." Unpublished manuscript, INSEAD, France 1985.

———. "The Relationship Between Return and Market Value of Common Stocks." *Journal of Financial Economics*, March 1981.

Banz, R., and W. Breen. "Sample Dependent Results Using Accounting and Market Data: Some Evidence." *Journal of Finance*, September 1986.

Bar Yosef, S., Sasson, and L.D. Brown. "Share Price Levels and Beta." *Financial Management*, Spring 1979.

Barry, C., and S. Brown. "Differential Information and the Small Firm Effect." *Journal of Financial Economics*, June 1984.

Basu, S. "Investment Performance of Common Stocks in Relation to Their Price-Earnings Ratios: A Test of the Efficient Market Hypothesis." *Journal of Finance*, June 1977.

————. "The Relationship Between Earnings' Yield, Market Value and Return for NYSE Common Stock." *Journal of Financial Economics*, June 1983.

Beaver, W., and D. Morse. "What Determines Price-Earnings Ratios?" *Financial Analysts Journal*, July–August 1978.

Beckers, S.; B. Rosenberg; and A. Rudd. "The January or April Effect: Seasonal-Evidence from the United Kingdom." Working paper, March 1983, BARRA, Berkeley.

Berges, A.; J. McConnell; and G. Schlarbaum. "The Turn of the Year in Canada." *Journal of Finance*, March 1984.

Berglund, T., and B. Wahlroos. "Further Evidence and an Explanation to Size-Related Anomalies in Asset Markets." Working paper, Swedish School of Economics and Business Administration, Helsinki, Finland.

Blume, M.E., and Frank Husik. "Price, Beta, and Exchange Listing." *Journal of Finance*, 1973.

Blume, M.E., and R. F. Stambaugh. "Biases in Computed Returns: An Application to the Size Effect." *Journal of Financial Economics*, November 1983.

Branch, Ben. "A Tax-Loss-Selling Trading Rule." *Journal of Business*, April 1977.

Brinson, G.; R. Hood; and G. Beebower. "Determinants of Portfolio Performance." *Financial Analysts Journal*, July–August 1986.

Brown, P.; A. W. Kleidon; and T. A. Marsh. "New Evidence on the Nature of Size-Related Anomalies in Stock Prices." *Journal of Financial Economics*, June 1983.

Brown, P.; D.B. Keim; A. W. Kleidon; and T.A. March. "Stock Return Seasonalities and the Tax-Loss Selling Hypothesis: Analysis of the Arguments and Australian Evidence." *Journal of Financial Economics*, June 1983.

Carleton, W., and J. Lakonishok. "The Size Anomaly: Does Industry Group Matter?" *Journal of Portfolio Management*, Spring 1986.

Carleton, W., and J. Lakonishok. "Risk and Return on Equity: The Use and Misuse of Historical Estimates." *Financial Analysts Journal*, January–February 1985.

Chan, K.C. "Can Tax-Loss Selling Explain the January Seasonal in Stock Returns?" *Journal of Finance*, December 1986.

Chan, K.C., "On the Return of the Contrairian Investment Strategy." Working paper, Ohio State University, Faculty of Finance, January 1987.

Chan, K.C.; N. Chen; and D. Hsieh. "An Exploratory Investigation of the Firm Size Effect." *Journal of Financial Economics*, September 1985.

Chan, K.C., and Nai-fu Chen. "Estimation Error of Stock Betas and the Role of Firm Size as an Instrumental Variable for Risk." Working paper, University of Chicago, November 1985.

Chang, E., and M. Pinegar. "Return Seasonality and Tax-Loss Selling in the Market for Long-Term Government and Corporate Bonds." *Journal of Financial Economics*, December 1986.

Clark, R., and W. Ziemba, "Playing the Turn of the Year Effect with Index Futures." Working paper, University of British Columbia, November 1986.

Clendenin, John. "Quality Versus Price as Factors Influencing Common Stock Price Fluctuations." *Journal of Finance*, 1951.

Cohen, K.; G. Hawawini; S. Maier; R. Schwartz; and D. Whitcomb. "Friction in the Trading Process and the Estimation of Systematic Risk." *Journal of Financial Economics*, August 1983.

Cohen, K.; G. Hawawini; S. Maier; R. Schwartz; and D. Whitcomb. "Estimating and Adjusting for the Intervalling Effect Bias in Beta." *Management Science*, January 1983.

Constantinides, G. "Optimal Stock Trading with Personal Taxes: Implications for Prices and the Abnormal January Returns." *Journal of Financial Economics*, March 1984.

Constantinides, G., and J.E. Ingersall, Jr. "Optimal Bond Trading with Personal Taxes." *Journal of Financial Economics*, September 1984.

Cooke, J., and M.S. Rozeff. "Size and Earnings/Price Ratio Anomalies: One Effect or Two?" *Journal of Financial and Quantitative Analysis*, December 1984.

Copeland, T. and F. Weston. *Financial Theory and Corporate Policy.* Reading, Massachusetts: Addison-Wesley, 1983.

Corhay, A.; G. Hawawini; and P. Michel. "Seasonality in the Risk Return Relationship—Some International Evidence." *Journal of Finance*, March 1987.

Cornell, B. "The Weekly Pattern in Stock Returns: Cash Versus Futures: A Note." *Journal of Finance*, June 1985.

Corner, D., and J. Matatko. "The Vienna Stock Exchange: Risk and Return in a Market with Discontinuous Trading." Working paper, presented at the *Third International Meeting of the French Finance Association*, June 1982 Orleans, France.

De Bondt, W., and R. Thaler. "Does the Stock Market Overreact?" *Journal of Finance*, July 1985.

————. "Further Evidence on Investors Overreaction and Stock Market Seasonality." Forthcoming in *Journal of Finance*, 1987.

Dimson, E. "Risk Measurement When Shares are Subject to Infrequent Trading." *Journal of Financial Economics*, June 1979.

Dimson, E., and P. Marsh. "Event Study Methodologies and the Size Effect: The Case of UK Press Recommendations." *Journal of Financial Economics*, September 1986.

Dorsman, A., and J.V.D. Hilst. "The Influence of the Calculation Interval on the Distribution of Returns at the Amsterdam Stock Exchange." Working paper, Universiteit van Amsterdam, Instituut voor Bedrijfseconomie en Accountancy, 1984.

Dowen, Richard J., and W. Scott Bauman. "A Test of the Relative Importance of Popularity and the Price-Earnings Ratio in Determining Abnormal Returns." *Journal of the Midwest Finance Association*, 1984.

Dyl, E. "Capital Gain Taxation and Year-End Stock Market Behavior." *Journal of Finance*, March 1977.

Edmister, Robert, and James Greene. "The Performance of Super Low-Priced Stocks." *Journal of Portfolio Management*, Fall 1980.

Elton, E., and M. Gruber. "Marginal Stockholders' Tax Rates and the Clientele Effect." *Review of Economics and Statistics*, February 1970.

Fama, E. "The Behavior of Stock Market Prices." *Journal of Business*, January 1965.

French, K. "Stock Returns and the Weekend Effect." *Journal of Financial Economics*, March 1980.

Fritzmeier, Louis. "Relative Price Fluctuations of Industrial Stocks in Different Price Groups." *Journal of Business*, 1936.

Fung, B.; R. Schwartz; and D. Whitcomb. "Adjusting the Intervalling Effect Bias in Beta: A Test Using Paris Bourse Prices." Salomon Brothers Center for the Study of Financial Institutions, New York University, 1983.

Gibbons, M., and P. Hess. "Day of the Week Effects and Asset Returns." *Journal of Business*, October 1981.

Givoly, D. and J. Lakonishok, "The Information Content of Financial Analysts' Forecasts of Earnings: Some Evidence on Semi-Strong Inefficiency. *Journal of Accounting and Economics*, Winter 1979.

Givoly, D., and J. Lakonishok. "Earnings Growth and the Firm-Size Anomaly." Working paper, Tel-Aviv University, January 1986.

Givoly, D., and A. Ovadia. "Year-End Tax-Induced Sales and Stock Market Seasonality." *Journal of Finance*, March 1983.

Goodman, David A., and John W. Peavy III. "Industry Relative P/E Ratios as Indicators of Investment Returns." *Financial Analysts Journal*, July–August 1983.

————. "The Significance of P/E Ratios for Portfolio Returns." *Journal of Portfolio Management*, Winter 1983.

Granger, C., and O. Morgenstern. "Spectral Analysis of New York Stock Market Prices." *Kyklos*, January 1963.

Grinblatt, M., and S. Titman. "A Comparison of Measures of Abnormal Performance on a Sample of Monthly Mutual Fund Returns." UCLA Graduate School of Management, Working paper, July 1986.

Grubel, H. "Internationally Diversified Portfolios: Welfare Gains and Capital Flows." *American Economic Review,* December 1968.

Gultekin, M.N., and B. N. Gultekin. "Stock Market Seasonality: International Evidence." *Journal of Financial Economics*, December 1983.

Hamon, J. "The Seasonal Character of Monthly Returns on the Paris Bourse." Working paper, presented at the *7th Annual Meeting of the French Finance Association*, Paris France, December 1985.

Harris, L. "A Transaction Data Study of Weekly and Intradaily Patterns in Stock Returns." *Journal of Financial Economics*, May 1986.

Haugen, R. *Modern Investment Theory.* Englewood Cliffs, N.J.: Prentice-Hall, 1986.

Hawawini, G. *European Equity Markets: Price Behavior and Efficiency.* NYU, Salomon Brothers Center for the Study of Financial Institutions, 1984.

Hawawini, G., and P. Michel. "The Pricing of Risky Assets on the Belgian Stock Market." *Journal of Banking and Finance*, June, 1984.

Hawawini, G.; P. Michel; and C. Viallet. "An Assessment of the Risk and Return of French Common Stocks." *Journal of Business Finance and Accounting*, Autumn 1983.

Hirsh, Y. *Don't Sell Stocks on Monday: An Almanac for Traders, Brokers and Stock Market Watchers.* Facts on File Publication, 1986.

Huberman, G., and S. Kandel. "A Size Based Stock Returns Model." Working paper, University of Chicago, July 1985.

Ibbotson, R.; R. Carr; and A. Robinson. "International Equity and Bond Returns." *Financial Analysts Journal*, July–August 1982.

Jaffe, J., and R. Westerfield. "Patterns in Japanese Common Stock Returns:

Day of the Week and Turn of the Year Effects." *Journal of Financial and Quantitative Analysis*, June 1985.

Jaffe, J.; D. Keim; and R. Westerfield. "Disentangling Earnings/Price, Size and Other (Related) Anomalies." Working paper, University of Pennsylvania, 1985.

Jansson, Solveig. "The Big Debate Over Little Stocks." *Institutional Investor*, June 1982.

Jensen, M. "Risk, the Pricing of Capital Assets and the Evaluation of Investment Portfolios." *Journal of Business*, April 1969.

————. "The Performance of Mutual Funds in the Period 1945–64." *Journal of Finance*, May 1968.

Kato, K., and J. Schallheim. "Seasonal and Size Anomalies in the Japanese Stock Market." *Journal of Financial and Quantitative Analysis*, June 1985.

Keim, D. "Size-Related Anomalies and Stock Return Seasonality: Further Empirical Evidence." *Journal of Financial Economics*, June 1983.

Keim, D. "Dividend Yields and Stock Returns: Implications of Abnormal January Returns." *Journal of Financial Economics*, September 1985.

————. "Dividend Yields and the January Effect." *Journal of Portfolio Management*, Summer 1986.

————. "The CAPM and Equity Return Regularities." *Financial Analysts Journal*, May–June 1986.

————. "Daily Returns and Size-Related Premiums: One More Time." *Journal of Portfolio Management*, Winter 1987.

Keim, D., and R. Stambaugh. "A Further Investigation of the Weekend Effect in Stock Returns." *Journal of Finance*, May 1984.

————. "Predicting Returns in the Stock and Bond Markets." *Journal of Financial Economics*, December 1986.

Kon, S. and F. "The Investment Performance of Mutual Funds: An Empirical Investigation of Timing Selectivity and Market Efficiency." *The Journal of Business*, April 1979.

Kon, S. and F. Yen. "The Investment Performance of Mutual Funds: An Empirical Investigation of Timing Selectivity and Market Efficiency." *The Journal of Business*, April 1979.

Lakonishok, J., and M. Levi. "Weekend Effects on Stock Returns: A Note." *Journal of Finance*, June 1982.

Lakonishok, J., and A. Shapiro. "Stock Returns, Beta, Variance, and Size: An Empirical Analysis." *Financial Analysts Journal*, July–August 1984.

————. "Systematic Risk, Total Risk, and Size as Determinants of Stock Market Returns." *Journal of Banking and Finance*, March 1986.

Lakonishok, J., and S. Smidt. "Volume, Price, and Rate of Return for Active and Inactive Stocks with Applications to Turn-of-the-Year Behavior." *Journal of Financial Economics*, September 1984.

————. "Trading Bargains in Small Firms at Year-End." *Journal of Portfolio Management*, Spring 1986.

————. "Volume for Winners and Losers: Taxation and Other Motives for Stock Trading." *Journal of Finance*, September 1986.

Lakonishok, J., and T. Vermaelen. "Tax Reform and Ex-Dividend Day Behavior. *Journal of Finance*, September 1983.

————. "Tax-Induced Trading Around Ex-Dividend Days." *Journal of Financial Economics*, July 1986.

Lessard, D. "World, National and Industry Factors in Equity Returns: Implications for Risk Reduction Through International Diversification." *Journal of Finance*, May 1974.

Levis, M. "Size-Related Anomalies and Trading Activity by U.K. Institutional Investors." Working paper, School of Management, University of Bath, 1985.

Levis, N. "Are Small Firms Big Performers?" *Investment Analyst*, April 1984.

Levy, H. "Equilibrium in an Imperfect Market: A Constraint on the Number of Securities in the Portfolio." *American Economic Review*, September 1978.

Levy, H., and Lerman, Z. "Testing P/E Ratios Filters with Stochastic Dominance." *Journal of Portfolio Management*, Winter 1985.

Lewellen, W.; K. Stanley; R. Lease; and G. Schlarbaum. "Some Direct Evidence on the Dividend Clientele Phenomenon." *Journal of Finance*, December 1978.

Litzenberger, R., and K. Ramaswamy. "The Effect of Personal Taxes and Dividends on Capital Asset Prices: Theory and Empirical Evidence." *Journal of Financial Economics*, June 1979.

————. "The Effects of Dividends on Common Stock Prices: Tax Effects on Information Effects." *Journal of Finance*, May 1982.

Miller, M., and F. Modigliani. "Dividend Policy, Growth, and the Valuation of Shares." *Journal of Business*, October 1961.

Miller, M., and M. Scholes. "Dividends and Taxes." *Journal of Financial Economics*, December 1978.

————. "Dividends and Taxes: Some Empirical Evidence." *Journal of Political Economy*, December 1982.

Nakamura, T., and N. Terada. "The Size Effect and Seasonality in Japanese Stock Returns." Nomura Research Institute, 1984.

Nicholson, S.F., "Price Earnings Ratios." *Financial Analysts Journal*, July—August 1960.

Officer, R. "Seasonality in Australian Capital Markets: Market Efficiency and Empirical Issues." *Journal of Financial Economics*, June 1975.

Osborne, M. "Brownian Motions in the Stock Market." *Operations Research*, March—April 1959.

Park, S., and M. Reinganum. "The Puzzling Price Behavior of Treasury Bills that Mature at the Turn of Calendar Months." *Journal of Financial Economics*, June 1986.

Peavy, J.W., and D.A. Goodman. "A Further Inquiry into the Market Value and Earnings Yield Anomalies." Working paper, Southern Methodist University, 1982.

Pettit, R. "Taxes, Transaction Costs and Clientele Effects of Dividends." *Journal of Financial Economics*, December 1977.

Pinches, George E., and Gary M. Simon. "An Analysis of Portfolio Accumulation Strategies Employing Low Priced Common Stocks." *Journal of Financial and Quantitative Analysis* June 1972.

Reinganum, M. "Misspecification of Capital Asset Pricing: Empirical Anomalies Based on Earnings Yields and Market Value." *Journal of Financial Economics* March 1981.

Reinganum, M. "A Direct Test of Roll's Conjecture on the Firm Size Effect." *Journal of Finance*, March 1982.

Reinganum, M. "The Anomalous Stock Market Behavior of Small Firms in January." *Journal of Financial Economics*, June 1983.

Reinganum, M., and A. Shapiro. "Taxes and Stock Return Seasonality: Evidence from the London Stock Exchange." *Journal of Business*, April 1987.

Rendelman, R.J.; C.P. Jones; and H. A. Latané. "Empirical Anomalies Based on Unexpected Earnings and the Importance of Risk Adjustments." *Journal of Financial Economics*, November 1982.

Richards, P.H. *U.K. and European Share Price Behavior: The Evidence.* London: Hogan Page, 1979.

Roberts, H. "Stock Market 'Patterns' and Financial Analysis: Methodological Suggestions." *Journal of Finance*, March 1959.

Rogalski, R.J. "New Findings Regarding Day of the Week Returns over Trading and Non-trading Periods." *Journal of Finance*, December 1984.

Rogalski, R.; and S. Tinic. "The January Size Effect: Anomaly or Risk Mismeasurement." *Financial Analysts Journal*, November—December 1986.

Roll, R. "A Possible Explanation of the Small Firm Effect." *Journal of Finance*, September 1981.

Roll, R. "On Computing Mean Returns and the Small Firm Premium." *Journal of Financial Economics*, December 1983.

Roll, R. "Vas Ist Das? The Turn of the Year Effect and the Return Premium of Small Firms." *Journal of Portfolio Management*, Winter 1983.

Rosenberg, B., and A. Rudd. "Factor-Related and Specific Returns: Microeconomic Determinants and Macroeconomic Correlates." *Journal of Finance*, May 1982.

Rosenberg, B.; K. Reid; and R. Lanstein. "Persuasive Evidence of Market Inefficiency." *Journal of Portfolio Management*, Spring 1985.

Rozeff, M.S. "The Tax-Loss-Selling Hypothesis: New Evidence from Share Shifts." Working paper, University of Iowa, April 1985.

————. "The December Effect in Stock Returns and the Tax-Loss Selling Hypothesis." Working paper, University of Iowa, May 1985.

Rozeff, M.S., and W.R. Kinney. "Capital Market Seasonality: The Case of Stock Returns," *Journal of Financial Economics*, November 1976.

Samuelson, P. "Proof that Properly Anticipated Prices Fluctuate Randomly." *Industrial Management Review*, Spring 1965.

Scholes, M., and J. Williams. "Estimating Betas from Non-Synchronous Data." *Journal of Financial Economics*, December 1977.

Schulman, E., "A Parable of Tulips." *Journal of Portfolio Management*, Spring 1986.

Schultz, P. "Transaction Costs and the Small Firm Effect: A Comment." *Journal of Financial Economics*, June 1983.

Schultz, P. "Personal Income Taxes and the January Effect: Small Firm Stock Returns Before the War Revenue Act of 1917: A Note." *Journal of Finance*, March 1985.

Schwert, G.W., "Size and Stock Returns, and Other Empirical Regularities." *Journal of Financial Economics*, June 1983.

Selden, G.E., "Year-End Selling: A Feature." *Magazine of Wall Street*, December 25 1920.

Smirlock, M. "Seasonality and Bond Market Returns." *Journal of Portfolio Management*, Spring 1985.

Solnik, B., "Why Not Diversify Internationally?" *Financial Analysts Journal*, July–August 1974.

Stevenson, R.A., and Rozeff, M. "Are the Backwaters of the Market Efficient?", *Journal of Portfolio Management*, Spring 1979.

Stoll, H.R., and R.E. Whaley. "Transaction Costs and the Small Firm Effect." *Journal of Financial Economics*, June 1983.

Strong, Robert A., "Do Share Price and Stock Splits Matter?" *Journal of Portfolio Management*, Fall 1983.

Tinic, S.; G. Barone-Adesi; and R. West. "Seasonality in Canadian Stock Prices: A Test of the 'Tax-Loss-Selling' Hypothesis." *Journal of Financial and Quantitative Analysis*, March 1987.

Tinic, S., and R. West. "Risk and Return: January Versus the Rest of the Year." *Journal of Financial Economics*, December 1984.

————. "Risk, Return and Equilibrium: A Revisit." *Journal of Political Economy*, February 1986.

Van den Bergh, W., and R. Wessels. "Seasonality of Individual Stock Returns: Recent Empirical Evidence for the Amsterdam Stock Exchange." Working paper, presented at the 10th Annual Meeting of the European Finance Association, Fontainebleau, France, September 1983.

Van den Bergh, W.M., and R.E. Wessels. "Stock Market Seasonality and Taxes: An Examination of the Tax-Loss Selling Hypothesis." *Journal of Business, Finance and Accounting*, Winter 1985.

Wachtel, S. "Certain Observations on Seasonal Movements in Stock Prices." *Journal of Business*, April 1942.

Wahlroos, B., and T. Berglund. "The January Effect on a Small Stock Market: Lumpy Information and Tax-Loss Selling." Discussion Paper Number 579, *Center for Mathematical Studies in Economics and Management Science,* Northwestern University, October 1983.

Wahlroos, B., and T. Berglund. "Anomalies and Equilibrium Returns in a Small Stock Market." Discussion Paper Number 58, *The Center for Mathematical Studies in Economics and Management Science*, Northwestern University, January 1984.

Wahlroos, B., and T. Berglund. "Stock Returns, Inflationary Expectations, and Real Activity: New Evidence." Discussion Paper Number 598, *The Center for Mathematical Studies in Economics and Management Science*, Northwestern University, May 1984a.

Zinberg, E., and J. Harrington. "The Stock Market's Seasonal Pattern." *Financial Analysts Journal*, January–February 1964.

INDEX